NML/FF

FIONA BECKETT'S
# CHEESE COURSE

FIONA BECKETT'S
# CHEESE COURSE
**STYLES ◆ WINE MATCHING ◆ PLATES & BOARDS ◆ RECIPES**

FIONA BECKETT

photography by Richard Jung

RYLAND PETERS & SMALL
LONDON • NEW YORK

**Author's Acknowledgements**

Many thanks to the cheese makers and cheese shops who have shared their knowledge and time, especially Ruaridh Buchanan of Paxton & Whitfield, who also supplied many of the cheeses for my tastings. Also to James Rackam of Emporia for providing some fascinating spirits and liqueurs for my pairing experiments, and my brilliant team at Ryland Peters & Small – commissioning editor Alison Starling, editor Céline Hughes, designer and fellow cheese obsessive Steve Painter, and photographer Richard Jung.

**Design, Photographic Art Direction
 and Prop Styling** Steve Painter
**Senior Editor** Céline Hughes
**Production Controller** Toby Marshall
**Art Director** Leslie Harrington
**Publishing Director** Alison Starling

**Food Stylist** Linda Tubby
**Indexer** Penelope Kent

Originally published in the UK in 2009

This edition published in 2013
by Ryland Peters & Small
20–21 Jockey's Fields
London WC1R 4BW
www.rylandpeters.com

10 9 8 7 6 5 4 3 2 1

ISBN 978 1 84975 424 8

A catalogue record for this book
is available from the British Library.

Printed and bound in China

For digital editions visit
rylandpeters.com/apps.php

## Notes

• All spoon measurements are level, unless otherwise specified.

• Ovens should be preheated to the specified temperature. Recipes in this book were tested using a regular oven. If using a fan-assisted oven, follow the manufacturer's instructions for adjusting temperatures.

• All eggs are medium, unless otherwise specified. Recipes containing raw or partially cooked egg, or raw fish or shellfish, should not be served to the very young, very old, anyone with a compromised immune system or pregnant women.

• Sterilize preserving jars before use. Wash them in hot, soapy water and rinse in boiling water. Place in a large saucepan and then cover with hot water. With the lid on, bring the water to the boil and continue boiling for 15 minutes. Turn off the heat, then leave the jars in the hot water until just before they are to be filled. Invert the jars onto clean kitchen paper to dry. Sterilize the lids for 5 minutes, by boiling, or according to the manufacturer's instructions. Jars should be filled and sealed while they are still hot.

# CONTENTS

# INTRODUCTION

If I was forced to choose just one food to eat for the rest of my life, it would have to be cheese. Not a day goes by when I don't sneak a nibble from the fridge, not a week when I don't make a cheese-based recipe. There's such an incredible variety of different cheeses – more than 1,000 in France alone – that I don't think I could ever become bored with it or fail to find an interesting new one to try.

And that's the problem for most people. So much choice, so much to learn. What on earth do you buy and how do you serve it, let alone find a wine to drink with it? These days, one's simply spoilt for choice.

This book is all about introducing you to cheese and styles of cheese you might not be familiar with, and helping you to enjoy them more. Discover how cheese is made and why it varies so much; how to create the perfect classic cheese board or a stylish, modern one with a twist; how to entertain with cheese (reinvent the wine and cheese party!), borrowing ideas from all round the world; how to introduce it into a romantic dinner for two or make it the focus of a barbecue or a brunch.

There's advice about how to pick the perfect wine for different types of cheeses (you'll find that white wine and sweet wines are a revelation), as well as other drinks, such as sherry, beer, cider and whisky – and even tea! You'll learn which breads are the best partners for different cheeses, and which biscuits. And finally, you'll get some ideas on how to make the ultimate cheese sandwich.

There are cheese ideas to match your mood and the season. Light, refreshing cheese plates for spring, vividly fruity ones for summer, mellow ones for autumn and glowingly warm ones for winter, including ideas for some show-stopping Christmas and Thanksgiving cheese boards.

There are recipes – mmmm, some really good recipes though I say so myself. If you're a macaroni cheese fan, you've got to try the Extra-crispy Macaroni Cheese (read the recipe on page 120 for the secret). There's my favourite new fondue made from cider and cheeses from the West of England where I come from; an Irresistible Italian Four-cheese Pizza and a tempting Tartiflette, the wickedly indulgent Alpine potato and cheese dish, a must for après-ski eating. Not to mention a couple of mouth-watering cheesecakes and some easy Raspberry and Ricotta Hotcakes and Double Cheese and Bacon Muffins to get your day off to the perfect start.

And then there's the basic tips you need to know: how to pick a cheese in perfect condition and how to make sure it stays that way. How to cut it, what to cut it with and how to use up the leftovers. And finally some new ideas for enjoying cheese without piling on the pounds – essential for all us cheese addicts!

I have to confess I have absolutely loved working on this book, which, thanks to designer Steve Painter and photographer Richard Jung, looks more beautiful than I could ever have imagined. I hope you enjoy reading and cooking from it as much as I enjoyed writing it.

LEFT *Selection of goats' cheeses*

# THE WONDERFUL WORLD OF CHEESE

THIS PAGE *Wedges of Brie*
LEFT *(Top and back) Isle of Mull, (bottom) Appleby's Cheshire*

# WHAT MAKES CHEESE TASTE SO DIFFERENT?

It's one of the miracles of cheese that one ingredient – milk – can be turned into so many different varieties of cheese. You really wouldn't believe it walking into the average cheese shop with its myriad different shapes, sizes and colours – or when you look at the line-up on a cheese board.

The process of making cheese can be incredibly simple but also highly skilled and labour-intensive. Many recipes are ancient ones going back several centuries. To make a good cheese, never mind a great one, you need to have had years of experience. And to taste the best cheeses in the world is like tasting a fine wine.

There are many variables, some of which are highly technical, but, keeping it simple, the most influential factors are the quality of the milk, the recipe the cheese is made from and how and for how long the cheese is matured.

## HOW CHEESE IS MADE

At its most basic, the process of making cheese couldn't be easier. You simply separate the solids in milk (the curds) from the liquid (whey) as you do in a simple recipe for labneh (see page 140). Of course, there's more to it than that otherwise all cheeses would have the same taste and texture. Some are simply moulded, others are pressed, some are heat-treated, some have bacteria introduced to turn them blue, some have rinds that develop naturally, others are washed or rubbed. Think of it like a whole lot of different recipes.

The easiest way I find to understand the process is to follow a single cheese through from start to finish as I did when I visited Keen's, a traditional producer of **West Country Farmhouse Cheddar**, a style of cheese that has its own Protected Designation of Origin (PDO). It's also one of only three cheeses which is entitled to use the description 'Somerset Artisan Cheddar'.

The milk, which is unpasteurized, comes from Keen's own herd of Friesian cows. First they introduce a starter culture which sours the milk and kicks off the process of separating it into curds and whey. They source this from

a laboratory that supplies cultures based on local microflora, to preserve the unique character of their cheese. Then rennet, an enzyme extracted from calves' stomachs, is added, again to accelerate the production of curds [1] [2]. (Vegetarian cheeses use other coagulants – see page 152.)

The milk goes through successive heating processes as each ingredient is added, finally forming a soft, sloppy mass called 'junket' which is chopped up to extract more liquid. Other softer cheeses are formed at this point but Cheddar goes through a unique process called cheddaring, which is fascinating to watch. The curds – by this stage a mass of buttercup-yellow granules – are pulled to the side of a large trough [3] to drain off the watery whey. As they're cut and re-cut [4], stacked and re-stacked [5], the texture changes, becoming firm and elastic. The weight of the layers pushes the blocks of cheese down, thereby extracting the rest of the whey [6].

When the cheddaring process is complete, the curd is passed through a mill to cut it into smaller, even-sized pieces. Salt – another crucial ingredient – is added to stabilize the curd, develop the flavour and to stop bacteria growing.

Then the cheese is put into moulds and left to drain [7] [8] [9]. Finally, the cheeses are smeared with lard [10] and triple-wrapped in muslin [11], a permeable coating that allows air to get to the cheese and moisture to continue to evaporate.

As the cheese ages, the surface gradually becomes colonized by moulds. The truckles, as the huge cheeses are called, are regularly turned and rubbed to ensure they mature evenly. You can see the rinds evolve from the multi-coloured spots on a cheese that is a few weeks old to the greyish, craggy surface of a mature one [12]. Most of Keen's Cheddars are stored for 10–12 months, although they age them for up to 2 years (see more on maturing cheese overleaf).

So what exactly makes other cheeses taste so different?

## OTHER WAYS OF MAKING CHEESE

There are many variations in the way that milk is handled that will result in different cheeses.

◆ Cheese makers may use different starter cultures to kick off the cheesemaking process or introduce bacteria that will create a certain type of rind, texture or flavour, as with bloomy-rinded cheese, such as **Brie**, cheese with holes, such as **Emmental**, and blues, such as **Stilton**.

◆ The amount the curds are stirred and the size they are cut will influence the final cheese – the more vigorous the stirring, the smaller the particles and the harder the cheese.

◆ Some cheeses are subject to higher temperatures or more heat processes than others. With **Mozzarella** and **Provolone**, the curds are left in hot water for some hours, then stretched or pulled into shape (a style known as 'stretched curd' or *pasta filata*).

◆ Cheeses are placed in different-shaped moulds (sometimes baskets) and may or may not be pressed. The longer a cheese is pressed and the greater the pressure, the more moisture is extracted and the harder the resulting cheese will be. Semi-soft and blue cheeses are not pressed.

◆ Salt can be added in different ways – as a brine, as in **Parmesan**, or directly on to the curds, as in **Cheddar**.

◆ A blue cheese will be pierced with needles to allow the characteristic blue veins to spread through the cheese.

◆ The rind may develop in different ways. Washed-rind cheeses, for example, may be rubbed with a brine solution or alcohol, such as wine, cider or marc (see page 18). White-rinded cheeses, such as **Brie**, can be sprayed to develop their characteristic white, velvety surface.

## THE MILK

Given that cheese consists of only one main ingredient, the character of the milk used is paramount and will vary from animal to animal, breed to breed, from one pasture to another, from winter to summer and from morning to evening.

## THE ANIMAL

Many animals produce milk for cheese we never get to taste – camel, reindeer and yak among them – but the most common are cows, goats and sheep. In general, cows' milk tends to be the richest in colour with a creamy, buttery taste; sheep's milk is more concentrated and tangy; goats' milk is fresher tasting and more citrussy. Cows' milk tends to make richer-coloured cheeses, while goats' and sheep's cheeses, which are more common across southern Europe and the Eastern Mediterranean, are a purer white or ivory colour. There are also variations between breeds. Jersey and Guernsey cows' milk, for example, is particularly rich and yellow.

At one time, you used to be able to say definitively that a certain style of cheese came from a certain type of animal but since cheese makers have become more experimental, there's a much greater crossover of styles, with Camembert-type cheeses being made from goats' milk, for example, or blues made from buffalo milk.

## THE PASTURE

The quality of the milk will also depend on the pasture the animal is grazing on – whether it is lush green grass, alpine, flower-filled mountain pastures or desolate scrub. In some cases you can actually pick up the flavour of herbs or of salt from animals which have grazed on pastures near the sea. You sometimes find the same flavours in cheese and wine from the same area. Both **Sancerre** and a **Crottin de Chavignol** share a mineral flavour, for example.

At some times of year the animals won't be out to pasture at all and will be eating hay and other winter rations, which will make their cheese less full-flavoured and aromatic.

The process of moving livestock from one type of pasture to another, from the valleys to the mountains, is called transhumance. That can be reflected in the name of the cheese. For example, there are different versions of **Beaufort**, called **Beaufort d'été** (summer Beaufort) and **Beaufort d'Alpage**, which is made in mountain chalets by the herdsmen who look after the cows.

## THE TIME OF YEAR

As just noted and rarely realized, cheese is seasonal and also – increasingly important with today's bizarre variations in climate – affected by the weather. Even in the spring or summer, a

traditionally productive time for cattle and other milk-producing animals, an unseasonal cold snap or a storm can affect the yield. Artisanal cheese – hand-made cheese made on a farm or by a small producer from locally sourced milk – isn't a standard product.

In general, soft cheeses like goats' cheese are at their best in the spring; semi-soft cheeses, such as **Brie** and **Camembert**, in the summer; and hard cheeses, such as **Cheddar** and **Stilton**, which mature for several months, in the winter. Some cheeses, such as **Vacherin Mont d'Or**, are only available at certain times of year – in this specific case from October to March. Others like **Gouda**, **Comté** or **Parmesan**, which are often matured for more than 18 months, show little seasonal variation.

## WHETHER THE MILK IS PASTEURIZED

The big issue in cheese making is whether milk should be pasteurized (heat-treated) or not. Large companies do it routinely to avoid any risk of contamination. Artisanal cheese makers tend to avoid it on the basis that it inhibits the individual character of their cheese, a view echoed by many ardent cheese lovers. In the end, it's a question of personal preference, although certain individuals, especially pregnant women and the elderly, are advised not to take the risk of eating untreated cheese (see page 152).

## MATURING CHEESE

You'd think the most important person so far as any cheese was concerned was the cheese maker. Well, surprisingly not! Equally, if not more important, is the role of the *affineur*, the person who matures the cheeses and ensures they reach the point of sale – shop counter

or restaurant – in perfect condition. The cheese maker and *affineur* may, of course, be one and the same person, and in the case of younger cheeses which don't hang around for more than a few weeks, often are. But more usually *affineurs* are attached to a cheese shop or, occasionally, to a restaurant (Max McCalman of Artisanal in New York and Christophe Demeyer of The Greenhouse in London being good examples). And in some cases where extended ageing of cheeses is the norm, as in a **Parmigiano-Reggiano** (**Parmesan**) or **Grana Padano** factory, there may be a whole team of *affineurs*.

Just like a cellar-master, they care for each cheese individually, turning it, brushing or washing its rind and checking its interior in the case of bigger cheeses until they decide the optimum moment has been reached to sell them. Some customers will want their cheeses more mature than others, just as some prefer their wines or steak aged for longer. The *affineurs* must make sure in the process that the cheeses don't dry out or attract the wrong kind of mould (artisanal Cheddar, for example, can develop veins like a blue cheese – fine for aficionados, but regarded with suspicion by the uninitiated).

Nowadays this process generally takes place in pristine storage rooms with laboratories on hand where the temperature and humidity are precisely controlled. When I visited one of France's most famous *affineurs*, Bernard Antony, who supplies cheese to many of France's top Michelin-starred restaurants, I was impressed by the fact that you could barely detect the smell of cheese but that each cheese was nonetheless full of character. Like other top *affineurs*, Bernard and his son Jean-Francois are most particular about the producers

they work with and select only those cheeses that meet their requirements.

## HOW LONG CAN CHEESE AGE?

In general, cheeses are aged for weeks or months rather than years but there are a few, such as **Parmigiano-Reggiano**, **Oude Gouda** and **Vieux Mimolette**, that can be aged for a good deal longer. In the main, these are large cheeses, as smaller cheeses would dry out too quickly.

What happens as cheese ages is that it loses moisture, concentrating the flavour. This generally makes them easier to match with wine, especially red wine, than younger, hard cheeses, as they don't tend to have as many volatile aromas and flavours. They also have the advantage of keeping better under domestic storage conditions than younger cheeses so you can store them for several weeks – if they last that long!

## WHY IS CHEESE SO EXPENSIVE?

It sometimes comes as a shock when I get presented with the bill in a cheese shop. After all, milk is not an expensive ingredient. However, it takes a surprising amount of milk to make a good-quality cheese – roughly ten times as much as the weight of the finished cheese. A **Beaufort** of 40–45 kilos, for example, will need about 500 litres of milk (around 110 gallons). It could take one cow around 10–12 days to produce that. Add to that the weeks and months of care and attention that goes into the cheese-maturing process and the long distances that many rare artisanal cheeses have to travel and you can see how the cost adds up. The only upside is that expensive cheeses tend to be more intensely flavoured so that you need to eat slightly less of them!

# THE DIFFERENT STYLES OF CHEESE: YOUNG UNRINDED CHEESES

There are a number of ways of categorizing cheese, some of them involving descriptions that are understood by producers and specialist cheese shops but are obscure to us, the public. What's the difference between a semi-soft and a semi-hard cheese, for example, or between a natural-rind and a washed-rind cheese? It is confusing. In my view the consistency of a cheese and the presence or absence of rind is the easiest way to look at cheese, together with how strong the flavour is.

## TASTE AND COMPARE

When you next go to the farmers' market, buy a goats' cheese at three different stages: a couple of days old, a week or 10 days old, and a month old. Taste and see the difference!

Young, unrinded cheeses are a popular style dominated by goats' and sheep's cheeses. When they're first made, they're light and moussey, just formed into a small flat disc or cylinder. A few days on they can be crumbled and a week or so later sliced. After a month they will have acquired a protective greyish coating of mould, often described as a 'natural rind'. Sometimes they're rolled in fresh herbs or ash.

Many first-time cheese makers and stallholders make these sorts of cheeses so there are a great many that are unnamed or named simply after the farm where they're made. Two better-known ones are the pyramid-shaped **Valençay** and Somerset **Tymsboro** and the herb-coated **Perroche** cheeses made by Neal's Yard.

Another well-known example is **Mozzarella**, which is heat-treated to create its characteristic springy, stretchy texture. It is known as a *pasta filata* (stretched curd) cheese in Italy (see page 12). Most Mozzarella these days is made from cows' milk though the most prized artisanal Mozzarella cheeses are made from the milk of water buffalo.

The by-product of Mozzarella is **ricotta**, which is made from the drained-off whey. It's one of a number of light soft cheeses that can be used both in sweet and savoury dishes. Others include **fromage frais** (otherwise known as **fromage blanc**), **quark** and the Greek cheese **Manouri**. Richer examples are **cream cheese** and **mascarpone**, which is used for the celebrated Italian dessert tiramisù. You can see what a straightforward process making a soft cheese is if you look at the recipes for labneh on page 140.

## SALTED CHEESES

Salted or brined cheeses, such as **Feta** share the characteristics of a young cheese, being crumbly and unrinded, but are often aged, at least in the best artisanal examples. The brine in which they are stored not only protects them from the air, which means they don't develop a protective crust or mould, but also gives them their characteristic salty taste. They are traditionally made from a mixture of different milks, usually sheep's and goats' milks.

*Clockwise from top left: ricotta, young button of goats' cheese, Perroche, fromage frais, buffalo Mozzarella*

**TASTE AND COMPARE**

Taste the difference between a creamy Brie de Meaux and an artisanal Camembert (pictured) or compare an unpasteurized cows' milk Camembert with a similar white-rinded goats' cheese, such as Tunworth.

# BRIE- AND CAMEMBERT-STYLE CHEESES

**Technically, the term for this style of cheese is 'bloomy-rinded', referring to the downy white surface that these cheeses acquire as they mature. The effect is induced by the introduction of a mould called *penicillium candidum*, which protects the surface of the cheese from other moulds.**

Unlike other cheeses, Brie and Camembert, which are also known as semi-soft cheeses, get softer and more voluptuous as they age rather than firmer and drier. When young they can be quite bland and chalky but as time goes on the centre develops a more unctuous creamy texture that can have a marked flavour of mushrooms. Except in very well matured cheeses, the rind remains quite palatable, adding a nutty flavour to each mouthful. As with other cheeses, unpasteurized versions tend to have a stronger flavour, Camembert generally being rather stronger than Brie. The best have the name of a region or town appended to them, for example **Camembert de Normandie**, **Brie de Meaux**, **Brie de Melun** and so on. Brie is generally made in much bigger wheels than Camembert.

Traditionally this style of cheese was made with cows' milk but many modern cheese makers, particularly in the US, are making them with goats' milk. Good examples are English **Tunworth** and Californian **Humboldt Fog**.

There are also white-rinded cheeses which are made to a slightly different recipe and in a different shape, such as **Chaource** from the Champagne region and **Gaperon** from the Auvergne, which is flavoured with garlic and peppercorns so it could be classified as a flavoured cheese (see page 25).

Pregnant women are advised not to eat bloomy-rinded cheeses because of the risk of listeria (see page 152).

*Explorateur (left), Finn (right)*

## ULTRA-CREAMY CHEESES

Some bloomy-rinded cheeses are exceptionally rich and creamy thanks to the addition of cream during the cheesemaking process. Referred to as double- and triple-crème cheeses, it's a style that's popular in France, which produces some of the most indulgent examples – **Explorateur**, **Brillat-Savarin** and **Pierre Robert** among them. **Finn** is a British cheese made in this style.

## A FRAGILE FLAVOUR

Once cheeses of this style have become mature, they deteriorate quite rapidly. The rind becomes progressively softer and stickier, acquiring a slightly ammoniac aroma and flavour that only hard-core cheese lovers will appreciate. If you buy an artisanal Camembert or Brie in perfect condition from a specialist cheese shop, it's better to eat it the same day, ideally picking it up at the last minute and keeping it in a cool place rather than in the refrigerator (though obviously don't leave it out for hours).

# WASHED-RIND AND SEMI-SOFT CHEESES

This category covers a wide range of cheeses that can range from mild to extremely pungent in flavour. And indeed one single cheese can cover that spectrum depending how long it is matured. A young Taleggio, for example, a washed-rind cheese from Lombardy in Italy, can be quite mild but an unpasteurized version can be overpowering if you're unused to it.

*Epoisses*

### TASTE AND COMPARE

Try washed-rind cheeses from different countries, e.g. French Munster or Epoisses, an English Stinking Bishop and an Irish Ardrahan. Or compare – if you dare – a relatively mild washed-rind cheese, such as Morbier with a really stinky one, such as Epoisses or Langres.

Many washed-rind cheeses were first developed in the monasteries. They are described as 'washed-rind' because the surface of the cheese is rubbed with a brine solution which promotes the growth of a bacterium. This breaks down the texture of the cheese, turning it soft and pliable rather than firm. (These cheeses are usually unpressed.)

It also develops their characteristic farmyardy aroma, sticky rind and rich array of colours, which range from sunset pink to deep orange. Beer, cider and marc (a distillate of grape skins and pips) can also be used to wash cheese. Well-known examples are **Epoisses**, **Langres**, **Munster** and **Reblochon** from France, **Chimay** from Belgium (produced by the brewery), **Appenzeller** from Switzerland and **Stinking Bishop** from Gloucestershire in England. There are also some fine Irish washed-rind cheeses including **Ardrahan**, **Durrus** and **Gubbeen**. **Cowgirl Creamery's Red Hawk** is one of the best in the US.

The 'bark' of washed-rind cheeses tends to be worse than their 'bite'. They may smell stinky but the taste is usually milder than you'd imagine. Typically they have a pliable, slightly springy 'paste' (what you usually call the centre of a cheese), which can be quite sweet and nutty in flavour. They are surprisingly good in cooking, giving a rich, full taste to recipes (see Tartiflette on page 112).

### SEMI-SOFT CHEESES

There are also semi-soft cheeses which are not washed. They share washed-rind cheeses' supple texture but don't have their pungent aroma. Examples are **Saint-Nectaire** and **Tomme de Savoie** (and similar French tomme or Italian toma-style cheeses).

Probably the ultimate washed-rind cheese so far as connoisseurs are concerned, **Vacherin Mont d'Or** is

**OPPOSITE** *Ardrahan (left), Durrus (right)*

a seasonal cheese only available from October to March. It doesn't have its fellow cheeses' pungency but makes up for it with a luxuriant, voluptuous texture that is accentuated by baking it in its box.

Confusingly, the French and the Swiss both lay claim to Vacherin, which is made to a similar recipe on both sides of the Alps. Despite the fact that the cheese appears to have been invented in France, the Swiss are entitled (much to the annoyance of the French) to use the name **Vacherin Mont D'Or** on their boxes. The French version is simply called **Mont D'Or** or, less commonly, **Vacherin du Haut-Doubs**.

*Vacherin Mont D'Or*

**TASTE AND COMPARE**

Compare a Beaufort (pictured, centre) or Comté with a mature farmhouse Cheddar, such as Keen's (pictured, left) and a Manchego (pictured, right). This is a nice little cheese board, come to think of it. You could also compare three different wines with it: a Savoie white, the traditional accompaniment for a Beaufort, a St Emilion with the Cheddar, and a Rioja Reserva with the Manchego.

# HARD CHEESES

How hard is a hard cheese? Some experts consider only rock-hard crystalline cheeses, such as Parmesan, to be truly hard but most of us would include semi-hard cheeses, such as Cheddar or Gruyère.

What cheeses made in this style tend to have in common is a process that involves cutting and heating the curds and pressing the just-formed cheese in order to expel as much of the whey as possible. They are hard in the sense that they contain less liquid than other cheeses, and firm as opposed to soft or pliable.

*Isle Of Mull*

As well as being pressed, hard cheeses may also be dipped in a brine solution to harden the rind (though not to promote bacteria as in a washed-rind cheese) and are generally aged for longer than other cheeses – in some cases for up to four years.

As with other styles of cheese, their taste and texture will depend on how long they are matured. A young **Cheddar** or **Gouda**, for example, will be milder and more pliable than an older one from which still more moisture has evaporated and which will have much more depth of flavour.

These are the main types of cheeses that fall into this category.

## WAXY SWISS-STYLE AND DUTCH-STYLE CHEESES

These include French and Swiss cows' milk cheeses, such as **Gruyère** (Swiss), **Beaufort** and **Comté** (both French). They have an ivory to yellow colour (depending on the season), a smooth, waxy texture and a hard rind. Although they are sometimes rubbed with a brine solution, the flavour is sweet and nutty

without the farmyardy elements of a washed-rind cheese or the 'bite' of a mature Cheddar. Aged versions of these cheeses, such as **Vieux Comté** and **Vieux Gruyère d'Alpage**, are some of the best the cheese world has to offer. Gouda-style cheeses, such as **Gouda** itself, **Coolea** from Ireland and **Teifi** from Wales also fit into this category, although they have a deeper colour and age in a different way, becoming more crystalline in texture. **Oude Gouda** can become almost as crumbly as **Parmigiano-Reggiano** (see below).

## CHEDDAR AND OTHER BRITISH TERRITORIAL CHEESES

Again there's variation within this group, from mild **Cheshire** and **Wensleydale** cheeses with their slightly crumbly texture to the powerful taste and firmer consistency of an authentic farmhouse **Cheddar**. Although Cheddar is made all over the world, the original cheese comes from Somerset and is made by a unique process which involves stacking the blocks of curd so that moisture is squeezed out, wrapping the cheese in

muslin, pressing it and ageing it in huge truckles (see pages 10–11).

## HARD SHEEP'S CHEESES

Just as goats' cheeses dominate the soft cheese category, so there are many sheep's cheeses in this section. Some are 'semi-hard', such as **Berkswell** from England, Spanish **Manchego** and **Ossau-Iraty** from the south-west of France. Some are harder and more crumbly, such as Italian **Pecorino**. They tend to be tangier, less creamy and more obviously salty than cows' cheese.

## VERY HARD CHEESES

These are the oldest cheeses you're likely to come across – cheeses that are so hard they have become almost crystalline and need to be shaved or grated rather than sliced. The best-known type by far is **Parmesan** or **Parmigiano-Reggiano**, but matured **Grana Padano** and **Pecorino** (also from Italy), **Sbrinz** from Switzerland, **Roomano** from Holland and **Vella Dry Jack** from California are similar in style.

# BLUE CHEESES

Some people shy off blue cheeses because they taste too strong but, as with other types of cheese, there is a wide range of flavours and textures.

Blue cheeses develop their characteristic blue veining when a harmless penicillin mould is added to the milk or curds. Once the cheese is formed, fine steel needles are inserted to expose the centre to oxygen, which enables the mould to spread throughout the cheese. Some cheeses are much bluer than others: a Cambozola or blue Brie, for example, will have very little veining, whereas the Spanish Cabrales is covered with blue streaks (see picture opposite, top right, which compares it with the barely blue Caradon Blue). In general, the greater the number of veins, the stronger the flavour.

Most blue cheeses are unpressed so are quite soft or crumbly in texture and fall into one of three groups.

## MILDER BLUES

The best-known cheeses that meet this description are blue Bries, such as **Cambozola** and **Gorgonzola dolce** (or **Dolcelatte** as it's also called). Although there is a touch of the characteristic saltiness and bitterness of blue cheese, this is offset by the creamy texture. There is, however, a trend towards milder blue cheeses with slightly more character, which has seen the introduction of interesting new blues like **Barkham Blue** (winner of many awards in the last six years), **Caradon Blue**, **Blacksticks Blue** and **Blue Monday**.

## MELLOW BLUES

The outstanding cheese in this style is undoubtedly **Stilton**, not only the most famous English blue but arguably the most famous English cheese after Cheddar. It is also one of the few to have a Protected Designation of Origin (PDO) – it can only be produced in the counties of Derbyshire, Leicestershire and Nottinghamshire. Some 'extra-matured' Stiltons pack quite a punch but in general this is a mellow, rich-tasting blue protected by its characteristic crumbly grey rind. Good producers are Colston Bassett and Cropwell Bishop. Since all Stiltons are now made from pasteurized milk, a new unpasteurized blue has come on the market called **Stichelton**, which tastes like Stiltons used to taste. Other comparable blues are the striking orange **Shropshire Blue**, creamy **Cashel Blue** from Ireland and **Fourme D'Ambert** from France.

## STRONG BLUES

This group includes the world's other best-known blues: **Gorgonzola** from Lombardy and **Roquefort**, the famous sheep's milk cheese from southern France – both are quite distinctive. **Gorgonzola**, though strong (or 'piccante') is rich and creamy, good for melting into pasta or risotto (see picture opposite, top left, comparing smooth, creamy **Gorgonzola** with mellow, crumbly **Stilton**). **Roquefort** is much sharper and saltier, a perfect partner to the equally famous sweet wine Sauternes. The Spanish also have a number of distinguished strong blues, such as **Cabrales** and **Valdeón**.

### CHEESE TIP

If you find a particular blue cheese too strong, you can always mix it with a little soft butter or cream to make a milder cheese spread and spread it on crackers as a little canapé to serve with drinks. Alternatively, mix it with other cheeses in a pasta bake or quiche.

### TASTE AND COMPARE

It's fascinating to compare the taste and texture of the world's best blues, so do try a Stilton, a Gorgonzola and a Roquefort together. Explore some blues you haven't tried, such as a Barkham Blue, a Bleu d'Auvergne and a Cabrales. Or take a look at the difference between a similar cheese made with different milks – Cashel Blue (cows' milk) and Crozier Blue (sheep's milk).

*Stilton and Gorgonzola*

*Cabrales and Caradon Blue*

*Cashel Blue*

*Barkham Blue*

# FLAVOURED CHEESES

**There are a remarkable number of flavoured cheeses nowadays. Many are disapproved of by cheese cognoscenti but flavouring cheese has perfectly respectable antecedents.**

Adding flavouring ingredients tends to be done to add visual interest and flavour to younger cheeses, although there are a few harder examples, such as **Majorero Pimentón**, a goats' cheese from the Canary Islands where the flavour (in this case pimentón or paprika) is rubbed into the rind. (Washed-rind cheeses are in effect flavoured by the type of alcohol that's rubbed into them but they tend not to be categorized by that flavour.)

Some, like the French cheese **Gaperon**, contain the flavours within the cheese, in this case garlic and peppercorns. Some cheeses, such as **Gouda** with cumin seeds, contain spices, others chillies, yet others herbs, such as sage or chives. There are also cheeses – which I have to admit I am less keen on – flavoured with fruits like apricots or cranberries, and even chocolate if you look hard enough.

Other cheeses, such as the British goats' cheese **Perroche** or the Corsican **Fleur du Maquis**, are rolled or coated with fresh or dried herbs or with spices, such as peppercorns. There is even one, **Hereford Hop**, which is rolled in toasted hops.

Still others get their flavour from the leaves in which they're wrapped. The Provençal cheese **Banon**, for example, is wrapped in chestnut leaves that are dipped in eau de vie, while **Cornish Yarg** is encased in the leaves of nettles. Other cheeses like **Caprini Tartufo** are infused with the flavour of truffles. You could even argue that **Vacherin Mont d'Or** (see page 18) is a flavoured cheese because of the strip of spruce bark that is wrapped round the cheese before it is put in its box.

Another way to imbue flavour is to marinate small or cut cheeses in herb-flavoured oil. You can buy these ready-made or make them yourself, as in the Marinated Feta with Herbs on page 141.

## SMOKED CHEESES

Like other ingredients, cheeses can be smoked, a technique that tends to suit firmer cheeses, such as **Cheddar** or **Gouda-style** cheese, although you can buy smoked Mozzarella (**scamorza**) and smoked blues, a speciality of the Rogue Creamery in Oregon.

*Scamorza*

# FIND YOUR TYPE OF CHEESE

*Beaufort*

*Mature Gouda*

As you will have seen from the preceding pages, there are many different styles of cheese and literally thousands of different cheeses – more than 1,000 in France alone! And given how different our taste buds are, it would be remarkable if we liked them all. Some people adore pungent, washed-rind cheeses, but to others their barnyardy smell is totally off-putting. Some love goats' cheeses. Others hate them (although often that turns out to be because they've only tried a very mature 'goaty' example).

Tastes evolve, so I would urge you to keep experimenting. If you think back to when you first tried coffee, you probably drank a mild, sweet, milky latte or cappuccino, then you might have dropped the sugar, reduced the milk and ended up an espresso lover. The same thing can happen with cheese. Here are some first steps to take you out of your comfort zone.

## IF YOU LIKE MILD CHEESE

You'll probably already like mild **goats' cheeses**, mild **Cheddar**, **Camembert**, **Brie**, mild Swiss and Scandinavian cheeses, such as **Emmental** and **Jarlsberg**, and **Mozzarella**.
**DO TRY:** Young goats' cheeses that are rolled in herbs or coated with ash. **Lancashire**, **Caerphilly** and other British regional cheeses, **Beaufort** (a wonderful French Alpine cheese – one of my favourites), **Boursault** (a creamy French cows' cheese) and a mild **Taleggio** (a good substitute for Mozzarella on pizza). You might even put a toe in the water with one of the milder blues (see page 22).

## IF YOU LIKE MELLOW CHEESE

You'll probably like a good **Cheddar**.
**DO TRY:** Exploring Cheddars from different producers – it's fascinating how different they are. I love a new organic Welsh Cheddar called **Hafod**, for example. There are also cheeses you'd enjoy made in a similar style, like **Lincolnshire Poacher**. If you've dismissed **Gouda** as being too bland, try a mature one – it's a revelation. And try younger versions of some of the wonderful new generation of Irish cheeses, such as **Gubbeen**, **Durrus** and **Ardrahan**.

*Explorateur*

*Berkswell*

*Stinking Bishop*

### IF YOU LIKE GOOEY, INDULGENT CHEESE

You'll probably be a fan of mature **Brie** and **Camembert**.
**DO TRY:** Triple-crème cheeses, such as **Explorateur** and **Brillat-Savarin**. There's also a meltingly soft ewes' milk cheese called **Le Pérail** that you almost need to scoop up with a spoon. (**Torta del Casar** is another.) And you haven't lived until you've tried a **Vacherin Mont d'Or** (see page 18).

### IF YOU LIKE SHARP CHEESE

You'll probably like **Feta** and **Pecorino** and may like salty blues, such as **Roquefort**.
**DO TRY:** Other hard sheep's and goats' cheeses. You probably know about **Manchego** but try other Spanish cheeses, such as **Zamorano** and **Roncal**, along with **Berkswell** from England. You should also look out for a fabulous hard goats' cheese called **Majorero** from the Canary Islands. And if you like **Roquefort**, you'll probably enjoy other sheep's milk blues, such as **Crozier Blue** from Ireland and **Beenleigh Blue** from Devon.

### IF YOU LIKE STRONG CHEESE

You'll probably like all those smelly French cheeses, such as **Livarot**, **Munster** and **Epoisses**.
**DO TRY:** Other washed-rind cheeses, such as **Stinking Bishop** from Gloucestershire and **Carré de l'Est**, an incredibly powerful (but delicious) beer-washed cheese from Northern France. (Wrap it up very well – even put it in a plastic box otherwise everyone will complain about the smell!) You should also look out for really well-aged hard cheeses, such as four-year-old **Parmesan**, **Roomano**, **Oude Gouda** and **Vieux Mimolette**, and strong blues, such as **Cabrales** and **Valdeón**.

# WHAT TO DRINK WITH CHEESE

THIS PAGE *Sauternes with Roquefort*
LEFT *Irish whiskey with (clockwise from top)*
*Cashel Blue, Ardrahan and Gubbeen*

# MATCHING CHEESE AND WINE

**If you asked your friends what food they most often associate with wine, I'm sure the majority would come up with cheese. But it's not always the perfect marriage it's held up to be. If you think for a moment about the average cheese board with five or six contrasting styles of cheese, it's a tall order to expect any one wine to match them all. And the better and more characterful the cheeses are, the harder it is – a dilemma for anyone who's both a cheese and a wine lover.**

Even with the less challenging situation of a single wine and a single cheese, you can find that a match misfires. The wine has only got to be a shade past its peak or the cheese allowed to mature a few days longer than recommended for a promising relationship to break down before it's even off the starting blocks.

I tell you this not to discourage you – there are some truly wonderful cheese and wine matches out there – but to explain why the cheese course is so often a disappointment with your favourite wine.

The first thing to be aware of is that white wines often pair better with cheese than red ones do. This stands to reason if you think about the fruits that generally accompany cheese, for example apples, pears, grapes and pineapple. Unoaked white wines in particular have a freshness and crispness that provide a perfect counterpoint to the rich, palate-coating texture of many cheeses.

Sweet wines too can work better with cheese than with a dry red, especially blues or other cheeses with a touch of bitterness that can clash horribly with the tannins in an oak-aged wine.

There are ways to encourage a red wine and cheese to match successfully and it's important to master them because your guests expect to enjoy the two together, but you need a bit of inside knowledge (see page 33).

A useful rule of thumb to help you make a successful match is that combinations of wine and cheese from the same region usually work. Good examples are **Gewurztraminer** and **Munster**, both from the Alsace region, **Chaource** and **Champagne**, **Crottin de Chavignol** and **Sancerre** from the Loire Valley, and a cheese fondue with a crisp dry **Savoie** or Swiss white. However, the Burgundian habit of serving **Epoisses** with fine local **red Burgundy** is not such a good idea. Personally, I think Epoisses is much better suited to **Marc de Bourgogne**, a grappa-like spirit (see page 18).

Another strategy you can employ is to 'build a bridge' between the cheese and the wine by introducing complementary ingredients that will facilitate the match. This, of course, has been done for years. The provision of bread (see page 67), crackers (see page 66), butter and fruit, such as grapes and apples, all modify the taste of the cheese, but nowadays there are many more options in the form of fruit pastes and jellies which can bring even more wines into play. Take a look at the section on Entertaining with Cheese (pages 48–83) for some more ideas.

You can also make your wine and cheese matching easier by serving your cheeses in peak condition. I don't mean that they shouldn't be well matured, simply that they should be freshly bought and carefully stored. With a few exceptions such as Parmesan-style cheeses, cheese is best bought little and often (see page 149). Most cheese is also more wine-friendly if you remove the rind, although if that is an aspect you enjoy, simply choose a stronger drink to accompany it.

Essentially, it's less a question of following a set of 'rules' than applying common sense. Milder cheeses are going to be much more accommodating with wine than stronger, more pungent ones. If you pair a **port** with a very young, moussey goats' cheese, it will overwhelm it. If you eat a strong blue cheese with a light white wine, it will strip the wine of its flavour. Like all food and wine matching, it's a question of getting the balance right.

*RIGHT Red wine with Stilton, butter, walnuts, walnut bread, oat biscuits and damson paste*

# RED WINE AND CHEESE

People want to drink red wine with cheese, full stop. It's such a long-held belief that the two go well together that it cannot easily be dislodged. But to avoid the almost inevitable disappointment that ensues, choose your cheeses and their accompaniments carefully.

There are three useful tips to bear in mind when choosing cheese to serve with red wine.

**1.** It's better to go for a hard rather than a soft or semi-soft cheese.

**2.** Remember that it is easier to match red wine with cooked cheese dishes than with uncooked cheese, especially when the dish features red wine-friendly ingredients, such as beef or mushrooms.

**3.** It helps to introduce other elements on the plate that will assist the match. Breads of character, such as walnut or sourdough (especially grilled), good farmhouse butter and cooked fruits, such as pears in red wine and cherry compote, will all help kick your wine into touch, as will a few marinated black olives, if you like them.

Oh, and don't be afraid to serve a single cheese on its own (see the 'hero' cheese board on page 55).

## CHEESES THAT WORK BEST WITH RED WINE

◆ Hard sheep's cheese, e.g. Italian **Pecorino**, **Manchego** and **Zamorano** from Spain, **Vermont Shepherd** from the US and British **Berkswell**: sheep's cheese is the most consistently successful match with red wine I've tried

◆ Well-aged cheeses that have a dry, crystalline texture, e.g. **Parmigiano-Reggiano**, aged **Gouda** and **Mimolette** and **Sbrinz** from Italy, Holland, France

*LEFT Red wine with Parmesan*

and Switzerland respectively. Younger versions of these cheeses will also match quite well.

◆ Mellow, medium-matured British territorial cows' cheeses, such as milder **Cheddar**, **Cheshire** and **Red Leicester**

◆ Red wine-washed cheeses such as the Italian **Ubriaco** and Spanish **Murcia al Vino** (but not white wine-, brine-, beer- or cider-washed ones)

◆ Mature or wrapped goats' cheeses like **Banon**

◆ **Provolone piccante**

## CHEESES TO AVOID WITH RED WINE

◆ Very oozy **Brie**- and **Camembert**-style cheeses

◆ Pungent washed-rind cheeses, such as **Epoisses** or **Langres**

◆ Strong blues, such as **Gorgonzola piccante** or **Roquefort**

## RED WINES THAT WORK BEST WITH CHEESE

◆ Aged Tempranillo-based reds, such as **Rioja Reserva and Gran Reserva**

◆ Mid-weight Grenache-based reds, such as **Côtes du Rhône** and modern Spanish **Garnacha**

◆ Mourvèdre-based reds, such as **Bandol** (one of my own personal favourites with cheese)

◆ Slightly 'porty' reds with rich brambly or figgy flavours, such as **Douro** reds, **Zinfandel** and **Amarone**, and southern Italian reds, such as **Aglianico** and **Negroamaro**

◆ There are circumstances in which other styles of red will work perfectly well with cheese too. Light, fruity reds, such as those from the Loire Valley and Beaujolais regions of France are good with goats' cheese, for example.

◆ Inexpensive fruity reds, such as **Chilean Pinot Noir**, **Merlot** and **Carmenère** can be enjoyable with a milder **Brie** or **Camembert**.

◆ A mature red **Bordeaux** can work well if none of the cheeses is too pungent. I recently successfully matched a six-year-old **Canon-Fronsac** with a cheese board of **Appleby's Cheshire**, **Waterloo** (a buttery semi-soft cows' milk cheese), **Berkswell** and **Cashel Blue**. The key was that the cheeses were all mellow and the wine had no harsh tannins.

◆ Even tannic young **Cabernet Sauvignon**, probably the most difficult red to pair with cheese, comes into its own with a steak or burger topped with melted blue cheese.

If you enjoy red wine and cheese but not always the two together, keep on experimenting! Look at the suggestions for berry-flavoured drinks on page 41 for more inspiration.

# WHITE WINE AND CHEESE

*Sauvignon Blanc with Perroche*

Once you've tried white wine with cheese, you'll never look back. The first experience is likely to be a glass of Sauvignon Blanc with a goats' cheese, an epiphany that should convert you at first sip. Once you've tried a crisp, fruity white with a fondue, or an Alsace Gewurztraminer with a pungent Munster you'll wonder why anyone drinks anything else.

The reason people are sceptical about accompanying cheese with white wine, as I've suggested on page 30, is that it seems slightly awkward to introduce a white wine at the end of a meal in which a full-bodied red has been served with the main course. You don't want to switch back to a light, crisp white and I don't blame you. But there are many lighter meals with which you might be drinking white and carry on doing so through the cheese course, or simple snacks where all you need to do is pull a bottle of white wine from the fridge.

## CHEESES THAT WORK BEST WITH WHITE WINE

◆ **Goats' cheese** is the white wine cheese par excellence whether it's a few days old, a week old or a month old (the latter can be interesting with older white wines). **Sauvignon Blanc** is the classic pairing but dry **Riesling** works well too.
◆ **Feta** and other white crumbly cheeses, such as **Caerphilly** and **Wensleydale**, also work well with crisp, fruity whites
◆ Alpine cheeses, such as **Gruyère**, **Comté** and **Beaufort**, and French **tomme** and Italian **toma** cheeses all suit white wines better than red. Smooth, dry whites with good acidity work well here, as do slightly aromatic whites, such as Alsatian **Pinot Gris**.
◆ Mild to medium-matured **washed-rind cheeses** suit aromatic wines, such as **Pinot Gris** and **Gewurztraminer**. More pungent examples are better with Trappist beers (see page 42) or stronger drinks (see pages 39 and 45–46).

## CHEESES TO AVOID WITH WHITE WINE

◆ **Blue cheeses** are not good with sharply flavoured dry white wines. They don't do many favours to aged cheeses, such as **Parmigiano-Reggiano**, either.

## WHITE WINES THAT WORK BEST WITH CHEESE

◆ Crisp, 'neutral' dry whites with good acidity, such as **Pinot Grigio** and other dry Italian whites and the Spanish grape variety **Xarel-lo**, are good with salads or antipasti with cheese and mild crumbly white British cheeses like **Caerphilly**
◆ Dry whites from Switzerland and the Savoie region of France work well with **Alpine cheeses** and **cheese fondues**
◆ Fruity dry whites, such as **Sauvignon Blanc** and Greek **Assyrtiko**, are brilliant with **goats' cheese** and Greek cheeses like **Feta** and **Halloumi**
◆ Aromatic off-dry whites, such as **Pinot Gris** and **Gewurztraminer**, pair well with washed-rind cheeses, such as **Munster**
◆ Dry Alsace and German **Rieslings** are a good alternative to Sauvignon Blanc with **goats' cheese**

◆ Smooth, dry whites, such as unoaked **Chardonnay** and **Pinot Blanc** work well with egg dishes that contain cheese, such as omelette and quiche
◆ White **Bordeaux** can be a fine match for an old **Comté**, while a barrel-fermented **Chardonnay** is a surprisingly good match for a **full-flavoured Cheddar** if you don't want to drink a port or a beer
◆ Southern French blends of **Roussanne**, **Marsanne** and **Viognier** are a good alternative to reds with sheep's cheeses, such as **Manchego**

## COOL NOT FREEZING COLD

We tend to think that all whites should be served well chilled but sometimes you can overdo it, particularly with more full-bodied or older whites whose opulent flavours can be dumbed down by being served too cold. While you can serve unoaked or aromatic whites like **Riesling** or **Sauvignon Blanc** at 8–10°C or after 2 hours in the fridge, fuller whites benefit from being served at 12–14°C or chilled for 1 hour 15 minutes –1 hour 30 minutes.

# ROSE AND CHEESE

Now that rosé is so popular, it's more than likely you will find yourself drinking it with cheese but, like other types of wine, it won't go with everything. Light, dry rosés such as Provençal rosés will go with much the same sort of cheese – particularly **goats' cheese** – as a fruity white would. A full-bodied, ultra-ripe **Cabernet** or **Syrah rosé** will behave more like a red, although you may find them more forgiving because of their fruitiness and absence of harsh tannins.

   Cheeses that go well with rosé include those that you might pair with berry-flavoured drinks (see page 41), particularly milder **Brie-** and **Camembert-style** cheeses, mild cheeses, such as **Chaource**, and creamy cheeses, such as **Finn** or **Explorateur**. Strong, dry rosés, such as those you find in Spain and southern France, are good with sheep's cheeses. Rosés are less successful with washed-rind and blue cheeses.

*Rosé with a mild Camembert*

# SWEET WINE AND CHEESE

**Why do sweet wines go so extraordinarily well with cheese? It's not just blues – although they are the outstanding match – but hard cheeses and washed-rinded cheeses too, as I discovered from a recent tasting I conducted: a superb Sauternes shone with almost every cheese we put with it, including a well matured Epoisses.**

Certainly the lusciousness of many sweet wines helps to make them shine: it coats the palate with syrupy sweetness and diminishes the effect of any bitterness in the cheese. Many have fruit flavours that are naturally complementary to cheese, such as grapes, peach, apricot and quince or, in the case of sweet red wines, plum and blackberries. And some have a crisp acidity that helps to counterbalance the semi-soft texture of washed-rind cheeses that can so easily defeat a red.

I know there's still a residual feeling that sweet wines are not somehow serious, or a needless indulgence at the end of a long meal, but I would urge you to give them a try. I promise that your guests will be impressed!

### CHEESES THAT WORK BEST WITH SWEET WINES

◆ Any blue cheese, whether it's crumbly like **Stilton** or **Fourme d'Ambert**, creamy like **Gorgonzola** or salty like **Roquefort** will find a sweet wine partner
◆ Powerful washed-rind cheeses, such as **Epoisses** or **Munster**, work as well with a sweet wine as they do with an aromatic one like **Gewurztraminer**. Try them with a wine that's both sweet and aromatic, such as a **vendange tardive** (a late-harvest sweet wine) or a late-harvest **Gewurztraminer**, and the effect should be sensational!
◆ Sheep's cheeses can be highly enjoyable with sweet wine. Try an **Ossau-Iraty-Brebis** with a **Jurançon** or **Pacherenc du Vic-Bilh** from the south-west of France
◆ Aged **Parmigiano-Reggiano** and **Gouda** are delicious with a sweet red wine like **Banyuls** or **Maury**
◆ **Cheddar** is good with **port** but also works amazingly well with sweet wines like **Sauternes**

### CHEESES TO AVOID WITH SWEET WINE

Nothing terrible happens but there are better things to drink with fresh young **goats' cheeses** and delicately flavoured cheeses, such as **Chaource**. I think they tend to dominate milder English regional cheese, such as **Caerphilly**, **Cheshire** and **Wensleydale**.

### SWEET WINES THAT WORK BEST WITH CHEESE

◆ **Sauternes** and similar sweet wines from the Bordeaux region, like late-harvest **Sauvignon Blancs**. The classic pairing is **Roquefort** but, as I mentioned before, they go with a much wider range of blues – and other cheeses.
◆ Richly flavoured sweet wines, such as **Tokaji** from Hungary, **Vin Santo** and the exotic **Passito di Pantelleria** from the tiny island just off the Sicilian coast. Again, they are great partners for a **blue cheese** but a good companion for a carefully chosen cheese board or plate that includes strongly flavoured cheeses.

*Sauternes with Roquefort*

◆ Sweet red wines, such as **Banyuls**, **Maury** and **Recioto** are interesting substitutes for port (see page 39) with **blue cheese** but they are also good with sheep's cheeses and aged cheeses, such as **Parmigiano-Reggiano** and **Mimolette**.
◆ Other sweet wines, such as southern French, Greek and Spanish **Muscat**, will do a good job. You can also find some spectacular matches for aged Alsace, Austrian or German **Riesling** although they do less well across the board. Matured **goats' cheese**, **Alpine cheese** and **hard sheep's cheese** work best.

### ADD A LUSCIOUS FRUIT

A good tip when you are pairing food and wine is to introduce an ingredient that will create a link or 'bridge' between the two, complementing the food and picking out flavours in the wine. With sweet wines and cheese, that could be a ripe peach or nectarine with a **Sauternes**, a few dried apricots (or nuts) with a **Tokaji** or a cherry compote with a sweet red wine like **port** (see more suggestions on pages 51–67).

## CHAMPAGNE AND CHEESE

It might surprise you to discover that Champagne can be excellent with cheese. I don't just mean with cheese canapés, such as gougères and crisp little cheese pastries whose 'umami' (savoury) flavours blend beautifully with the biscuity flavour of a mature sparkling wine. It also works well with a slightly chalky cheese, such as a **Chaource** (a classic match), a delicately flavoured young goats' cheese, or a double- or triple-crème cheese. If you're lucky enough to have a vintage Champagne on your hands, it will be sensational with an aged **Parmigiano-Reggiano** or a **Vacherin Mont d'Or**. For a Valentine's treat, try serving a truffle-infused cheese, such as a **Caprini Tartufo**, or a heart-shaped **Cœur de Neufchâtel** with a **rosé Champagne** – a wonderful way to woo any cheese lover! (See also Cheese for Two on page 56.)

# PORT, SHERRY AND OTHER FORTIFIED WINES AND CHEESE

Port is so firmly associated with cheese that other fortified wines don't get a look-in, but sherry, Madeira and similar wines can be just as successful. People can be a little reluctant to bring out a strong wine at the end of dinner, so I prefer to offer these pairings as an aperitif or an imaginative, between-meals snack – a late afternoon alternative to tea or even an indulgent mid-morning offering for weekend guests if lunch is running late! A small glass of port or sherry and a nibble of cheese also make a nice nightcap if you've eaten early (but not too much of either or you may have a sleepless night!)

**CHEESE TIP**

You can enhance a match between cheese and a fortified wine by bringing in accompaniments that reflect the flavours in the wine: olives and almonds in the case of a fino sherry; raisins, dried figs, dates or ready-to-eat prunes with stronger, sweeter sherries; a damson or cherry compote with a brambly, late-vintage port.

ABOVE *Malmsey Madeira with Roquefort, dried figs and raisins*
LEFT *Fino sherry with Manchego, olives and Marcona almonds*

### CHEESES THAT WORK BEST WITH DRY, TANGY WINES (FINO AND MANZANILLA SHERRY AND SERCIAL MADEIRA)

◆ Hard Spanish and Basque sheep's cheeses, such as **Manchego** and **Ossau-Iraty** (especially with accompanying green olives and almonds)
◆ Aged goats' cheeses
Less good with rich, creamy cheeses.

### CHEESES THAT WORK BEST WITH DRY, NUTTY WINES (DRY AMONTILLADO, PALO CORTADO AND DRY OLOROSO SHERRIES, VERDELHO MADEIRA AND 20-YEAR-OLD TAWNY PORT)

◆ Hard Swiss-style cheeses, such as cave-aged **Gruyère**, **Beaufort** and **Comté**, **Cheddar**, **Red Leicester**
◆ **Gouda-style** cheeses, mature **Parmigiano-Reggiano** and **Sbrinz**
Less good with young, moussey goats' cheeses.

### CHEESES THAT WORK BEST WITH PALE, SWEET WINES (CREAM SHERRIES AND WHITE PORT)

◆ Mild blues, such as **Gorgonzola dolce (Dolcelatte)**, **Cambozola** and other **blue Brie**
◆ Mild, hard sheeps' cheeses

Less good with mature **Cheddar** and strong blues.

### CHEESES THAT WORK BEST WITH SWEET, NUTTY WINES (10-YEAR-OLD AND SOME 20-YEAR-OLD TAWNY PORTS)

◆ Mellow blues, such as **Stilton**
◆ Medium-matured **Cheddar** and **Gouda-style** cheeses, **Mimolette**
◆ Milder washed-rind cheeses
Less good with young goats' cheeses, **Feta** and other crumbly white cheeses.

### CHEESES THAT WORK BEST WITH PLUM- AND BERRY-FLAVOURED WINES (LATE-BOTTLED VINTAGE AND VINTAGE PORT)

◆ Blue cheeses, especially **Stilton**
◆ **Cheddar**
Less good with young goats' cheeses but overall a pretty versatile all-rounder.

### CHEESES THAT WORK BEST WITH SWEET, RAISINY WINES (SWEET OLOROSO AND PEDRO XIMENEZ SHERRIES, AND BUAL AND MALMSEY MADEIRAS)

◆ Tangy **Cheddar** and strong blues, such as **Roquefort** and **Cabrales**, especially with raisins, figs or dates
Less good with young goats' cheeses, **Brie**, **Camembert** and garlic-flavoured cheeses.

# APPLE-FLAVOURED DRINKS AND CHEESE

**One of the best ways to grasp how cheese and drink pairing works is to focus on a single ingredient. Think about the various drinks that contain that flavour and how they might match with different cheeses.**

A good example is apple, which turns up in a wide range of drinks. At one end of the spectrum you have fresh-tasting **apple juice**, which is well suited to daytime drinking and to young, fresh cheeses. At the other end you have an oak-aged drink, such as **Calvados** or **Applejack**, a full-strength spirit that

better suits after-dinner occasions and strong cheeses that can defeat red wines. In between these you have a range of apple-based drinks of different strengths – **cider**, **Pommeau** or other apple-based aperitifs and **apple eaux de vie**, some of which can be turned into cocktails. You'll be surprised what

### APPLE JUICE

My own preference is for cloudy, **unfiltered artisanal apple juices,** which have a much truer, pure apple flavour. These are ideally suited to fresh young **goats' or sheep's cheeses**, particularly in salads or light vegetable quiches. To dress up the apple juice, served it chilled in a jug with fresh apple slices, slices of lemon and whole mint leaves.

### CIDER

Ciders vary in style from mass-produced ciders that taste like lager, to draught scrumpy, taking in various degrees of sweetness in between. Let's pitch for a middle-of-the-road, **dry farmhouse cider**, which is wonderful with a ploughman's lunch of **Cheddar** and apple chutney. Sparkling **Normandy cider** is a great terroir-based match for **Camembert**.

successful matches can be made. For a drinks party with a difference why not arrange a cheese and apple evening, laying on different types of cheese and matching drinks? Or taste different ciders with different cheeses, served alongside a variety of apples from the farmers' market? It's great to be able to introduce your guests to new flavour combinations and it really gets people talking.

## BERRY-FLAVOURED DRINKS AND CHEESE

You could perform a similar exercise with berry-flavoured drinks. Line up some **cranberry or pomegranate juice** (good with **cream cheese**), a **cherry or raspberry beer** (with **berry-topped cheesecake**), **Pinot Noir** (with a young **Brie**) and a **cherry liqueur** or a **vintage character or late-bottled vintage port** (with **blue cheese**).

## CHEESE TIP

You need to think about the strength of both the drink and the cheese. A medium-matured Camembert, for example, would pair well with a Normandy cider, whereas a very well matured, unpasteurized one would pair better with a Pommeau or a Calvados.

## APPLE APERITIFS

There is a wide range of apple-flavoured aperitifs. Some, like **Pommeau**, are simply stronger versions of cider (or weaker versions of apple brandies if you like); others are more like an **apple-flavoured eau de vie**. For a strikingly different drink, serve ice-cold shots of vivid **Apple Sourz** in martini glasses with crostini topped with **goats' cheese** and diced apple.

## APPLE BRANDIES

Apple brandies like **Calvados**, **Applejack** and **Somerset cider brandy** are particularly good companions for strong artisanal cheese, such as well-matured **Camembert fermier** or a powerful washed-rind cheese like **Pont-l'Evêque** (both from Normandy). Go for younger brandies rather than ones labelled 'hors d'age' where the apple flavour is less evident.

# BEER, CIDER, PERRY AND CHEESE

*Ale with Lincolnshire Poacher*

It's hard for us wine lovers to accept, but beer and cider are every bit as good as wine with cheese, and in some cases even better. If you've ever tried a Camembert with cider or a 'stinky' washed-rind cheese with a strong Belgian Trappist ale you'll know exactly what I mean. When I wrote my beer and food book *An Appetite for Ale* a couple of years ago, I was blown away by the combinations I discovered. The one problem is that there's still a bit of a stigma about bringing beer to the dining table but please don't be put off. With the increased interest in craft beers, I'm sure that will soon change.

## CHEESES THAT WORK BEST WITH BEER

Some cheeses that cause problems with wine are outstanding with beer.

◆ Washed-rinded cheeses, such as **Epoisses** with strong, dark **Belgian Trappist beers** and French **Bières de Garde**. Some monasteries, like **Chimay**, produce both beer and cheese.

◆ Strong **Cheddar** and similar cheeses, such as **Lincolnshire Poacher** and other full-flavoured British territorial cheeses like **Lancashire**, pair well with traditional British ales

◆ Full-flavoured blues, such as **Stilton** and **Blue Vinney**, are excellent with **barley wine** (see below), **porter** and **Triple Bock**

◆ Mature **Gouda** and **Mimolette** are good with a strong, dark **Belgian beer** or a full-flavoured **saison-style brew**

## CHEESES TO AVOID WITH BEER

I wouldn't match fresh young goats' cheeses with a robust porter or a strong blue with a lager.

## BEERS THAT WORK BEST WITH CHEESE

◆ **Barley wine**, which is in fact a super-strong ale, is the port of the beer world.

A great choice for a winter cheese board.

◆ **Porter** is a good all-rounder with classic British cheeses, especially blues. It can also be good, by contrast, with rich, creamy cheeses like **Boursault**.

◆ **Oak-aged beer**, a relatively new category, which works particularly well with strong **Cheddar** and Cheddar-style cheeses

◆ **Amber ales and lagers**, also known as **bières ambrées**, work well with hard sheep's cheeses, such as **Ossau-Iraty** and **Berkswell**, and with **Gouda-style** cheeses. They're also a good partner for baked cheese dishes like lasagne.

◆ **Fruit beers**, especially cherry and raspberry-flavoured beers (**Kriek** and **Frambozen**) are great with white-rinded cheeses, especially **Brie**, and with **goats' cheese** salads

◆ Fresh, citrussy Belgian-style **witbier** (or **bières blanches** as they're also known) are fantastic with **goats' cheese** and mild British territorial cheeses, such as **Caerphilly** and **Wensleydale**

◆ You might think it would lead to a smoke overload but **smoked beer** works well with **smoked cheese**. It is also good with Alpine cheeses, such as **Gruyère** and **Comté**.

◆ **Chocolate and coffee beers** are stunning with **tiramisù**!

## COOKING WITH BEER AND CHEESE

Beer is a good constituent of cheese recipes, most famously Welsh Rarebit (see page 146), but also beer and cheese soups. Or you can make a fondue along the lines of the Cheddar and Cider Fondue on page 106.

## CIDER, PERRY AND CHEESE

Having a more limited range of flavours, **cider** and **perry** make less versatile companions to cheese than beer but where they do work, for example with **Camembert** (see page 40), they work exceptionally well. Lacking the alcoholic strength of stronger ales, they are less successful with blues and pungent washed-rind cheeses.

◆ Enjoy **cider** with milder British cows' cheeses, such as **Caerphilly**, **Cheshire** and medium-matured **Cheddar**, with milder **Gouda-style** and Swiss cheeses and with hard sheep's cheeses (slices of apple will enhance the pairing)

◆ **Dry perries** pair particularly well with **goats' cheese**

*Cider with Camembert*

# WHISKY AND CHEESE

Of all the foods that can show off a fine malt, cheese is by far the most congenial (to me, at least, although chocolate and whisky lovers would probably want to argue their corner!) Of course, as with other spirits, there's the issue of introducing a new drink at the end of a meal, but as with fortified wine, I think it's an experience that works better on its own than as part of a meal. A couple of oatcakes or oat biscuits (see page 136), smothered with Caboc or other creamy cheese, and a fragrant, floral malt or light, blended whisky are a thoroughly appealing snack.

*Irish cheese board: Irish whiskey with (clockwise from top) Cashel Blue, Ardrahan and Gubbeen*

If you want to make a real impact, you could create a terroir-based cheese board of Scottish cheeses with Scotch whisky or Irish cheeses with an Irish one. For the Scottish board, I suggest **Lanark Blue**, an **Isle of Mull** or **Loch Arthur Cheddar** and **Bishop Kennedy**, which is actually washed in whisky. For the Irish board, see picture above: **Cashel Blue**, **Ardrahan** and **Gubbeen** (oak-smoked if possible).

## CHEESES THAT WORK WELL WITH WHISKY

◆ Characterful blue cheeses, such as **Roquefort**, **Lanark Blue** (a great match with a peaty Islay whisky like **Lagavulin**, see below) and mature **Stilton**
◆ Cream cheeses, from mild to double- or triple-crèmes like **Explorateur** work well with lighter, floral malts, as does the oatmeal-coated **Caboc**
◆ **Cheddar** is good with richer, fuller whiskies that are aged in sherry casks, like **The Macallan**
◆ **Smoked cheeses** work well with most whiskies other than intensely peaty ones

**LEFT** *Whisky with Caboc and oatcakes*

## CHEESES TO AVOID WITH WHISKY

Steer away from more delicate cheeses that will be overwhelmed by the level of alcohol, for example young goats' cheeses. And there are better drink partners for semi-soft cheeses, such as **Vacherin Mont d'Or**.

## WHISKIES THAT WORK WELL WITH CHEESE

◆ Lighter blends and floral whiskies, such as **Dalwhinnie** and **Glenkinchie** are the best styles to go for with creamy cheeses. Also good with **Parmigiano-Reggiano** and aged goats' cheeses.
◆ Full, rich whiskies, whiskies aged in sherry casks, **Bourbon**: mature **Cheddar** and **Gouda-style** cheeses, plus mellow blues, such as **Barkham Blue** and **Stilton**
◆ Peaty 'island' whiskies: this is the style that really stands out with cheese, especially with strong blues, such as **Roquefort**, and salty cheeses, such as barrel-aged **Feta**. You can also try these whiskies with **Cheddar** and milder washed-rind cheeses.

## DO YOU NEED TO DILUTE WHISKY TO DRINK IT WITH CHEESE?

Purists would say 'no' but it's very much a matter of taste. I like to reduce the alcohol of cask-strength whiskies, which can be up to 60 percent, and often add a splash of water to other malts to release their aromas and flavours. It's more common to dilute blended whiskies than malts but if you feel a whisky is a little 'hot', do add a splash.

## OTHER OAK-AGED SPIRITS

Other oak-aged spirits are surprisingly good with cheese, especially **Calvados** and other apple brandies – the best match by far for a tricky-to-handle mature **Camembert** or its Normandy cousin, a mature **Pont-l'Evêque** (see page 41). Other brandies, such as **Cognac** and **Armagnac**, work well too, especially with washed-rind cheeses although I marginally prefer their less well-known counterpart, **Marc de Bourgogne**, an excellent match for an **Epoisses** or a **L'Ami du Chambertin**. You might also try a **Cheddar** or mature **Stilton** with a dark rum. I've enjoyed the latter with a **Bristol Classic Rum**.

# OTHER DRINKS THAT PAIR WELL WITH CHEESE

**There are many other possible pairings with cheese. Here's just a taster.**

### FRUIT-FLAVOURED EAUX DE VIE, SCHNAPPS AND 'BRANDIES'

Typically unoaked, the intense fruit flavours of **eaux de vie**, **schnapps** and **aquavit** can work exceptionally well with cheese, my favourite pairing being **Pecorino** (or other sheep's cheese) and **Poire William**, the pear-flavoured eau de vie from Alsace. Fruit 'brandies' and flavoured gins, such as **apricot brandy**, **cherry brandy** and **sloe and damson gin**, tend to be less strong but equally appealing. Try **apricot brandy** with a full-cream cheese, such as **Boursault**, **cherry brandy** with **Brie** or hard sheep's cheese and **sloe** or **damson gin** with **Stilton** (see opposite).

### FRUIT WINES

Although made from fruits other than grapes, fruit or 'country' wines can work in a very similar way to red table wine with the advantage that they lack the tannic structure that can make red wines such a problem with cheese. I particularly like **elderberry** and **blackberry wine** as an alternative to **port** with **blue cheese**, and **Japanese plum wine** (**umeshu**) with creamy **Brie**.

### GRAPPAS AND UVE

Like **marcs** (see page 45), **grappas** are made from the skin, pips and stalks that are discarded from the wine-making process, but are less often oaked. **Uve**, like **eaux de vie**, are made from whole grapes. I particularly enjoy grappas and uve with Mediterranean sheep's

cheeses, such as the herb-coated **Fleur du Maquis** from Corsica.

### GIN AND GENEVER

A surprising inclusion, you may feel, but the botanicals in **gin** and its Dutch counterpart, **genever**, play particularly well with strong washed-rind cheeses like **Epoisses** and **Munster** in much the same way as a **Gewurztraminer**. (My most exciting cheese pairing while writing this book was **Plymouth Gin** and a ferociously strong northern French cheese called **Carré de l'Est**.)

### APERITIFS

Aperitifs are a particularly French and Mediterranean phenomenon that cover a wide range of drinks, from **Pommeau**, the rather attractive by-product of **Calvados** that goes similarly well with **Camembert** and washed-rind cheeses (see pages 40–41), to cherry-flavoured **Guignolet** (delicious with **Brie**) and aniseed-flavoured drinks like **pastis**, **ouzo** and **raki** which tend to go well with salty sheep's cheeses, such as **Feta**, alongside other mezze. Off-dry **vermouths**, such as **Chambéry** and **Lillet Blanc**, are also pleasant with milder cheeses and cheese spreads.

### SAKE

Another unlikely-sounding pairing but, thanks to its absence of tannins, **sake** fares much better than wine with many cheeses. (One New York cheese shop, Murray's, holds regular sake and cheese

tastings.) Try it with **Gruyère** and **Emmental**, with **tomme-style** cheeses and with hard goats' and sheep's cheeses, such as **Manchego**.

### MEAD

Although there is a passionate following for mead (a beverage fermented from honey), it's hard to find specialist retailers. However, if you do come across a bottle, buy some and try it as a substitute for dessert wine with a mild to medium-strong **blue cheese**.

### TEA

While not particularly to my taste, tea and cheese also has its advocates, especially the combination of strong, earthy **Pu'erh** with washed-rind cheeses. And if you're not a whisky drinker but like the smokiness, try a cup of the equally pungent **Lapsang Souchong** tea rather than an Islay whisky with **blue cheese**.

### SOFT DRINKS

Almost all the flavours you find in wine you can find in soft drinks – and they will work with similar cheeses. A fragrant **elderflower cordial**, for example, is perfect with **goats' cheese**; and **apple and pear juices** work with similar cheeses to cider (e.g. mild English regional cheeses, such as **Cheshire**). Meanwhile, **red grape, pomegranate, cranberry and other berry-flavoured juices** pair with just the same cheeses as light fruity reds, especially mild **Brie**.

# ONE CHEESE, MANY POSSIBILITIES...

Just to show how there is no one single answer to a cheese pairing conundrum, here are 12 different possibilities with a single cheese. I've picked Stilton because it's a relatively easy cheese to match even though it's a blue, and you can take the pairing in a number of directions.

### SWEET, BERRY-FLAVOURED DRINKS

**Port (vintage or late-bottled vintage)**
The classic Stilton pairing – festive and warming. The velvety smoothness of a vintage port matches the rich creaminess of the cheese perfectly.

**Elderberry wine**
An old-fashioned drink but an underrated one that works better than most red table wines.

**Sloe or damson gin**
Lighter in alcohol than port but just as intensely flavoured. One of my favourites and always brought out at Christmas.

### RICH, RAISINY AND NUTTY DRINKS

**10- or 20-year-old tawny port**
Having been aged in oak casks, these acquire a nuttier, more toffee-ish flavour than ruby and vintage ports, which may appeal if you find those styles too sweet. Enhance the match with a selection of nuts and some figs or dates.

**Sweet oloroso sherry or Madeira**
With their sweet Christmas cake flavours, sweet oloroso sherries and Bual and Malmsey Madeira make just as enjoyable a partner for Stilton as port.

### FRANGELICO

This sweet Italian hazelnut liqueur makes a way-out pairing for all you culinary thrillophiles out there.

### SUMPTUOUS DESSERT WINES

**Sauternes**
With its luscious citrus and honey flavours, you might think Sauternes was too light to go with Stilton but it's a brilliant match.

**Tokaji**
Hungarian Tokaji has a different flavour profile – rich orange peel, dried apricot and marmalade flavours. Another personal favourite.

**Vin Santo**
Italian wine and British cheese? The warm, rich flavours of Vin Santo make it a great combination. The more expected Italian blue, Gorgonzola, would work too.

### FULL-FLAVOURED, OAK-AGED SPIRITS

**A rich sherry cask-matured malt**
Whisky is underrated as a partner for cheese. Many different styles would work with Stilton – including island whiskies – but this is the one I prefer.

**Armagnac or Cognac**
Each has its devotees but I'm a fan of the lesser-known and beguilingly varied Armagnac. Serve a few of the finest prunes, pruneaux d'Agen, on the side.

**Demerara rum**
Rarely paired with food but a fascinating partner for a mellow blue cheese, such as Stilton.

*Pecorino, Sardinian carta da musica and Vermentino*

# ENTERTAINING WITH CHEESE

*Brie, cherries and Guignolet*

# A CLASSIC CHEESE BOARD

**For any cheese lover, the idea of being able to work your way round a selection of contrasting cheeses is one of the best ways of indulging your passion. As a wine lover, I have some reservations about this but there are times when you just can't beat it.**

The classic approach in putting together a cheese board is to aim for a contrast of textures, tastes and shapes. Mild to strong, rounds and wedges, light against dark, soft and hard – it's about making an aesthetic impact as much as a gustatory one.

A classic cheese board will contain a cheese from one of each of the main styles. You can obviously leave out any you don't like or which you think will not go down well with your guests (washed-rind cheeses being the most likely candidates) but you should try to make sure there's something for everyone.

## A CLASSIC SELECTION

Serve a young, fresh-tasting **goats' cheese** (see page 14); a white or bloomy-rinded cheese, such as a **Brie** or a **Camembert** (see page 17); a hard cheese like a **Cheddar** (see page 21); and a blue, such as a **Stilton** (see page 22). You could also add a washed-rind cheese (see page 18); a sheep's cheese (see pages 14 and 21); or a cheese flavoured with herbs (see page 25).

Traditionally, this choice would have been drawn predominantly from Britain and France but there are now so many exciting new cheeses from elsewhere in the world that there are many alternative countries from which to find them. You could include cheeses from your own neighbourhood and from halfway across the globe.

The picture opposite shows a classic board with something for everyone – from top left, a classic **Camembert**, **Tymsboro** (an ash-coated goats' cheese from Somerset), **Colston Bassett Stilton**, **Montgomery's Cheddar** (also from Somerset), **Epoisses** (a washed-rind cheese from Burgundy), and **Sarriette de Banon** from Provence. The classic way to present them would be clockwise in order of flavour intensity (Tymsboro, Sarriette, Camembert, Cheddar, Epoisses and Stilton) but I much prefer to arrange the board to show off the cheeses' different shapes, colours and textures. You could, however, eat them in this order, sticking to the more easy-going cheeses (Tymsboro, Sarriette, Cheddar and Stilton) if you were drinking red wine – see page 33 for why red wine can cause problems with cheese. Overall I think the best match for this particular selection would be a **vintage tawny port** or, you might be surprised to hear, a good **Sauternes** (see page 36). Remember the more mature a cheese is, the more difficult it can be to find a precise wine match so do consider other drinks (see page 46).

## AN IRISH CHEESE BOARD

I suggest an **Adrahan** (washed-rind cheese), a **St Tola** (a soft goats' cheese), a **Coolea** (Gouda-style cheese), a **Gabriel** (hard cows' cheese) and a **Cashel Blue**.

## AN ITALIAN CHEESE BOARD

This might include a **Gorgonzola**, a semi-soft **Taleggio**, **Pecorino Sardo** (hard sheep's cheese) and a **Caprini Tartufo** (truffle-infused goats' cheese).

## AN ANIMAL-LED CHEESE BOARD

While it is traditional to mix cheeses from different animals – goat, cow and sheep – it's possible with the multitude of new cheeses that are being produced to base a board purely on sheep's or goats' cheeses, or a mixture of the two – a boon to those who find themselves intolerant to cows' milk (see page 152).

A modern British example of a non-cows' milk cheese board might include **Little Wallop** (the 'celebrity' goats' cheese produced by former Blur guitarist Alex James), **Tunworth** (a Camembert-style goats' cheese), a **Berkswell** (an excellent hard English sheep's cheese) and **Lanark Blue** (a fine sheep's cheese from Scotland).

## A SURPRISE SELECTION

As you become more knowledgeable about cheese, it's fun to mix the familiar and the unfamiliar. Try serving a new discovery from the farmers' market or a rare **Spanish or Portuguese cheese** alongside an old favourite that you know everyone loves (a great **Cheddar** or a creamy **Brie**, for example).

**LEFT** *(Clockwise from top left) Camembert, Tymsboro, Colston Bassett Stilton, Montgomery's Cheddar, Epoisses, Sarriette de Banon*

# CONTEMPORARY CHEESE BOARDS

Even ardent cheese lovers tend to be quite conservative about the way they serve cheese, sticking to the classic formula of having several different types of cheese from different countries and serving them on wooden boards (see page 51). But over the past few years I've come across many new and different ways of presenting cheese. Restaurants nowadays are much more imaginative about the surfaces they use, the way they cut cheeses and the accompaniments they put with them, and these innovative ideas can suggest new and exciting ways to serve cheese at home.

At Alain Ducasse's eponymous restaurant at The Dorchester in London, for example, I was served a 'tray' of four different cheeses with accompanying relishes: **Valençay** goats' cheese with sweet pepper relish; **Montgomery's Cheddar** with poached grapes and Muscat wine jelly; a three-year-old **Vieux Comté** with a paste made from hazelnuts and vin jaune (a matured, sherry-like French white wine); and **Stilton** with Mostarda di Cremona (preserved fruit infused with mustard oil, typically from Cremona in northern Italy).

At the Auberge du Paradis, an innovative French restaurant in Saint-Amour-Bellevue in the Beaujolais region of France, the cheeses – **Valençay**, **Brillat-Savarin** and **Vacherin Mont d'Or** with a dusting of paprika – arrived on a slate board with a spoonful of mirabelle (plum) purée and a cumin seed-crusted breadstick.

You don't have to attempt such fancy presentation but you can gain inspiration from them and adapt them to create a cheese board that will be a real talking point for your guests. Here are some ways to do it.

### DIFFERENT SURFACES

There's no reason why a cheese board, which is merely shorthand for a selection of cheeses, should actually be a wooden board. It could be a tray, a basket, a series of tiles, glass or a slate.

Slate is my own personal favourite. It's sophisticated and elegant and looks wonderful against the whites and greyish blues of goats' cheeses, white rinded cheese and blues. Think in terms of ash-covered pyramids, such as **Tymsboro**, a bloomy-rinded cheese like **Waterloo**, **Morbier** with its distinctive streak of ash running through the middle and one of my favourite modern blues, **Barkham Blue**. Add a contrasting selection of pale celery and charcoal crackers and maybe a violet-coloured velvety fresh fig or two and you've got a strikingly beautiful presentation.

### DIFFERENT SHAPES

I'm thinking less of the shapes of the cheeses themselves here but the way you cut or scoop them (a spoon is an underrated implement when it comes to dealing with gooey cheeses like the runny sheep's milk **Le Pérail**!)

Hard cheeses, such as **Parmesan**, can be shaved with a cheese slicer or special Parmesan knife; washed-rind cheeses can be cut into fine slices (though don't do this too far in advance of bringing it to the table or it will dry out). For more ideas on cutting and displaying cheese, see page 151.

Don't be afraid to upturn cheeses either. Wedges look dramatic propped on their base, point upwards: take a look at the presentation on the websites of some of the more innovative cheese retailers, such as The Fine Cheese Company, Neal's Yard Dairy and New York's Artisanal (see Cheese Suppliers and Websites on page 158).

### FEWER CHEESES

Smaller selections have significant advantages. They're cheaper, obviously, you're more conscious of the flavours of each individual cheese but, lastly and most importantly, you can design them to accompany a particular style of wine.

It's a strategy that I think works particularly well with red wine, which tends to clash horribly with certain cheeses (see page 33) or with awkward customers such as washed-rind cheeses or strong blues.

If you wanted to carry on drinking the fine red you had served with the main course, you could serve a firm-slicing **goats' cheese**, a **Pecorino** and a

**RIGHT** *(Clockwise from top right) Morbier, Waterloo, Barkham Blue and Tymsboro with charcoal crackers and fresh figs*

*Cheese and sherry flight, from left: Oude Gouda and dry oloroso,*
*Gorgonzola and cream sherry, Manchego and fino*

piece of aged **Gouda**, for instance. Alternatively, if you had a delicious sweet wine, you might want to lay on a selection of three contrasting blues (see page 36).

And there's no reason why your accompaniment shouldn't be a beer. Pick three contrasting hard cheeses, say a **Comté**, a **Gouda-style cheese** and a **Cheddar** and serve them with a **barley wine** or a strong **Belgian Trappist beer** (see page 42).

## WINE AND CHEESE 'FLIGHTS'

A brilliant idea for wine and cheese lovers pioneered by the innovative Artisanal cheese shop and bistro in New York, is to arrange a wine and cheese 'flight'. This is a selection of three different wines and cheeses served in small quantities to taste and compare. Usually the wines will be of a similar type, for example three or four wines made from the same grape – say Syrah or Shiraz – or four wines of different types from the same wine region, say the Loire. You can look at Artisanal's current suggestions on their website (www.artisanalbistro.com) or invent your own. The idea applies equally well to other drinks. Why not try a sherry and cheese flight using some of the suggested pairings on page 39, a whisky and cheese flight (see page 45) or an apple-flavoured drinks and cheese flight (see pages 40–41).

## FOLLOW THE SEASONS – AND THE WEATHER

Cheese, as I've already pointed out on pages 12–13, is seasonal, but perhaps even more importantly, from the point of view of the cheese lover, it needs to adapt to the weather. Just as with other foods, one is drawn to different cheeses depending on whether it's cold or hot and sunny. (In general, these temperatures coincide with winter and summer but the climate is so variable nowadays that you could find yourself basking in the autumn or freezing in the early spring!)

I tend to prefer lighter, younger, fresher-tasting cheeses like goats' and sheep's cheeses when it's hot; and stronger, more mature cheeses, such as washed-rind cheeses, aged hard cheeses and blues when the temperature drops below freezing (and Swiss cheeses but that's a question of mood as much as taste).

For a warm-weather cheese board you could offer a goats' cheese, a hard sheep's cheese and a jar of Marinated Feta with Herbs (see page 141) with a glass of rosé; on a chilly night you could serve an **Appenzeller**, a **Taleggio** and a **Gorgonzola** – perhaps with a warming glass of **grappa** or **schnapps**! See also the suggestions for seasonal cheese plates on pages 60–61 and for Festive Cheese on page 83.

## A LOCAL CHEESE BOARD

I've already suggested basing a cheese board on a specific country (see page 51), as it's easy enough to find five or six contrasting cheeses. But if you want to serve entirely local cheeses – and that's a nice thing to do – it's better to think of serving two or three, preferably with a locally produced drink (beer, cider or fruit wines may be easier in some areas than wine), a locally made chutney or relish and some locally baked (or home-baked) bread. If you have a particularly good local cheese maker, you could base your cheese board on their cheeses.

## AN ADVENTUROUS CHEESE BOARD

This is one for friends who are really into cheese. Try to find some obscure cheeses they'll never have heard of or source them from a country whose cheeses are less well known – like Canada, Sweden, Spain and Portugal. Cheeses I've tasted recently that fall into this category include **Tiger Blue** from British Columbia, **Svecia** from Sweden, **Ilha Graciosa** from the Azores and **Afuega'l pitu** from the Asturias region of Spain. That should impress any cheese buff!

## A 'HERO' CHEESE BOARD

If you have found an exceptional cheese, there's an argument for making it the only one on the board so that your guests really have the opportunity to appreciate it without the flavour of other cheeses getting in the way. It also makes it more likely that you will finish it and avoid wasting what may be an expensive buy.

Against that you could argue that there may well be people present who might not like that type of cheese or who may not be able to tolerate it for dietary reasons (see page 152) so you probably have to know your guests well to do this. I wouldn't be inclined to offer a very strong blue, for example, as my only cheese (although a Stilton at Christmas is traditional), nor a pungent washed-rind cheese.

Good cheeses to feature in a solo role are a well-matured (but not over-runny) **Brie de Meaux** or **Camembert**, a fine **Cheddar**, a visually striking cheese, such as **Mimolette** or **Morbier** with its distinctive line of ash running across its middle, or an aged **Parmigiano-Reggiano**, a choice that will flatter a fine red wine. A **Vacherin Mont d'Or** also deserves to stand on its own.

# CHEESE FOR TWO

**We tend to think in terms of large numbers for cheese boards but it's surprising how often you serve it just for two. Cheese is an indulgent treat which will make any cheese lover feel pampered and is an easy-to-prepare part of a romantic dinner.**

One's instinct when catering for just two people is simply to buy less cheese but while that can be a good strategy with the right cheese (see the 'hero' cheese board on the previous page), if you're entertaining, particularly if it's a romantic occasion, it could seem ungenerous.

What I like to do is create a miniature cheese board, which could be on a small butcher's block or a slate. Rather than putting out big pieces of cheese, I usually cut them into one-portion wedges or slices and put two of each on the board.

*Rosé Champagne with Cœur de Neufchâtel and strawberries*

## A GENEROUS CHEESE BOARD FOR TWO

You could have two **goats' cheese buttons**, two wedges of **Camembert** or other white-rinded cheese, two slices of **Beaufort** and two radicchio leaves topped with a spoonful of a soft blue cheese, such as **Gorgonzola** or **Cashel Blue**. Perch two pots of fruit compote or chutney alongside, or a couple of Grape Jellies (see page 145), add a few grapes or a couple of fresh figs, some small home-baked rolls or pre-cut slices of raisin bread and some rustic artisanal breadsticks and you've got a very pretty-looking board indeed.

## A ROMANTIC CHEESE PLATE FOR TWO

For a more romantic occasion, you could serve the heart-shaped **Cœur de Neufchâtel** or a truffle-infused cheese, such as **Caprini Tartufo**. Alternatively, slice a small, deep, round cows' cheese into horizontal slices and sandwich with fine shavings of black truffles, press together, wrap in clingfilm and leave in the fridge overnight for the flavour of the truffles to infuse the cheese. Serve with **rosé Champagne**.

## A SUMMER CHEESE BOARD FOR TWO

For a summer date, think of partnering cheese and berries: indulge your partner with fine wedges of **Chaource**, wild strawberries and a glass of **pink fizz** or treat him or her to a romantic breakfast of Raspberry and Ricotta Hotcakes (see page 128).

## A MINI-FONDUE FOR TWO

Sometimes the simplest ideas are the most delicious! You can bake a whole **Camembert** and it will taste like the most fabulous fondue. Simply take the cheese out of its box and remove the wrapping. Replace the cheese in the box and lightly rub the surface with a cut clove of garlic, pierce the surface of the cheese with a skewer in a few places, then put the lid of the box back on. Bake it in a preheated oven at 200°C (400°F) Gas 6 for about 25 minutes until the cheese is gorgeously gooey. Serve with crusty bread and breadsticks or tiny boiled new potatoes to dunk into the molten filling.

*Brie, cherries and Guignolet*

# CHEESE PLATES

**The difference between a cheese plate and a cheese board is not the surface on which it's presented but the fact that each person's cheese is served individually rather than put out in the middle of the table to share. In my view it's a better way of handling the cheese course, particularly in the middle of a dinner party. You don't have to buy as much cheese, you can create a perfect balance of ingredients on the plate, it works better with wine or other drinks and it looks great too.**

A cheese plate is also a stylish way to enjoy a small snack of cheese. A hunk of cheese cut from the fridge and an apple may satisfy the hunger but if you're offering it to guests you want to make it look a bit more elegant.

You can borrow any of the ideas from elsewhere in the book – for example the Contemporary Cheese Boards on page 52, the Seasonal Cheese Salads on pages 94–95 or the country-based suggestions on page 51 – and scale them down for a cheese plate, but one of the best ways of creating interesting combinations of flavours is to look to the season for inspiration (see overleaf).

You can also create a plate to match a particular type of wine or other drink. You'll find many suggestions in the What to Drink with Cheese chapter on pages 28–47.

**LEFT** *Poire William with Pecorino and pears*

The best way to discover great pairings is to experiment. If you find a delicious new cheese, try different drinks with it. If you buy a beautiful bread or some unusual biscuits, ask the shop what cheese they would recommend with them. If you bring home a new wine, pour half a glass and try it out with any cheeses you have in the fridge. Here are some of the unusual combinations I've discovered in this way.

◆ **Morbier** is kinder to **red wine** than many washed-rind cheeses
◆ Smoked oatcakes make a great base for a creamy cheese, topped with a curl of wafer-thin smoked salmon and accompanied by a mild **whisky**
◆ **Gin**, of all drinks, is a good counterfoil to a pungent **washed-rind cheese**
◆ **Elderflower** is as sympathetic to **goats' cheese** as **Sauvignon Blanc**

### IN THE SPRING

Spring is the time we all want to enjoy the first of the new season's produce, which happily pairs perfectly with the new young cheeses. Decorate your cheese plates with leaves and herbs, accompany them with crisp, fresh white wines and celebrate the end of winter.

◆ Serve a grilled slice of **goats' cheese** marinated in oil with a herb salad or steamed or charred asparagus. Alternatively, scatter fresh goats' cheese or a white crumbly cheese, such as **Wensleydale**, over a few mixed salad leaves. Perfect with **Sauvignon Blanc** or an aromatic **Belgian wheat beer**.
◆ Serve two contrasting **goats' cheeses** for comparison – one very young and still soft, the other firmer and more mature with rosemary-flavoured crackers and some herb-marinated olives. Try a crisp **rosé** this time.
◆ Do as the Italians do and serve cooked, peeled broad beans, fine slices of **Pecorino** and shards of Sardinian *carta da musica* with a glass of **Vermentino** *(pictured above)*
◆ Another simple but sophisticated Italian idea for an aperitivo: strips of focaccia, **Parmesan** shavings and a glass of **Prosecco**

### IN THE SUMMER

Take advantage of the wealth of fresh fruit and vegetables to show off your cheeses: fresh berries, watermelon, peaches, apricots, tomatoes and peppers. Don't be afraid to introduce a touch of spice. Chilli and garlic work well with cheese.

◆ Serve thinly sliced **sheep's cheese** with grilled peppers and almonds as a mini tapas plate with a glass of **fino sherry**. Or do as the Basques do and serve it with a cherry compote and a glass of **fruity red wine**.
◆ Serve individual ploughman's platters with a good chunk of **Cheddar**, thickly carved ham, a dollop of chutney, an apple, some crusty bread and traditional **English ale or cider**
◆ Serve a mini antipasto plate with slices of fennel, salami, **mozzarella** and grilled artichokes or slow-roasted tomatoes and breadsticks. Drink a **light Italian red or white** with this.
◆ Plate up wedges of watermelon, crumbled **Feta**, pumpkin seeds, olive oil and balsamic vinegar *(pictured above)*
◆ Serve a creamy cheese, such as **Explorateur**, **Robiola** or **Brillat-Savarin** with a peach and a glass of **dessert wine**
◆ A show-stopper: a wedge of **Brie**, some fresh cherries and a small glass of **Guignolet** or a **Belgian cherry beer**

## IN THE AUTUMN

Autumn is the prime time for some of the ingredients that go best with cheese: apples, pears, grapes, figs and nuts.

◆ Serve a wedge of ripe **Camembert** with sautéed apple slices and a glass of **Pommeau**
◆ A classic but none the worse for it: thin slices of **Manchego** with membrillo (quince paste) and a **palo cortado sherry**
◆ Try ripe pears, **Pecorino** and chilled **Poire William**: clean and simple
◆ Fresh or grilled figs with **Gorgonzola** and a glass of **Maury**, a sweet red wine from the Roussillon region of France *(pictured above)*
◆ Give your cheese an Indian twist: try a washed-rind cheese like **Munster** scattered with roasted cumin seeds, served with mango chutney and strips of warm naan bread. Serve with **Gewurztraminer** or a hoppy **Indian pale ale**.
◆ Two different **blues** – one cows' milk, one sheep's milk – with a mixed leaf and walnut salad drizzled with a walnut oil dressing. Surprisingly good with a full-bodied **Chardonnay**.
◆ A cheese and jelly plate: Grape Jellies (see page 145) and **Brie**. Sauternes jelly and **Stilton**.

## IN THE WINTER

Winter cheese plates can take advantage of all the preserved fruits that are available – luscious big raisins, dates and figs – as well as the array of fortified wines and liqueurs that come out at this time of year (see also Festive Cheese on page 83).

◆ A Spanish trio of **Cabrales** (one of the world's best blues), raisins and **Pedro Ximénez sherry**
◆ A striking combination: **Fourme d'Ambert**, toasted walnut bread, poached kumquats and **Grand Marnier**
◆ **Stilton**, oatmeal biscuits and **sloe or damson gin** – a great combination and just as good as port
◆ Dorset **Blue Vinney** and **barley wine** (a strong ale). Strong ales are wonderful with blue cheese.
◆ Two stylish Italian ways of serving **Gorgonzola**. Drizzle with chestnut honey and serve with griddled panettone and **Vin Santo**, or serve with a thin wedge of panforte and a glass of **Marsala**.
◆ Fine slices of **Mimolette** or **Oude Gouda** with Medjool dates, dried figs, nuts and **tawny port** *(pictured above)*
◆ A nibble of good farmhouse **Cheddar**, Brazil nuts and sweet **oloroso sherry**

*Summer berries with ricotta and honey*

*Leerdammer (raised), Emmental (bottom), Tilsit (back)*

*Prosecco with different types of cheese bagel*

# BREAKFAST AND BRUNCH

**If you're not used to it, the idea of starting the day with cold meats and cheeses may seem strange but in many countries such as Holland, Germany and Scandinavia it's quite traditional. It's certainly a sustaining way to 'break your fast' and much easier than the traditional cooked breakfast to prepare for a crowd.**

Mild, sliceable cheeses, such as **Tilsit**, **Emmental** and **Leerdammer** work better at this time of day than stronger washed-rind cheeses or blues, which provide the palate with rather too emphatic a wake-up call! Light, mild, soft cheeses, such as **ricotta** and **fromage frais** are also good at breakfast time, especially with fruit. A big bowl of low-fat fromage frais and another of mixed strawberries, raspberries and blueberries makes a lovely centrepiece for a summer breakfast table or brunch. Alternatively, an idea I picked up from The Old Convent hotel in Ireland is to make fresh fruit 'martinis' by spooning fromage frais into martini glasses and topping up with a selection of freshly cut fruit.

Treat weekend guests to a batch of the delicious Raspberry and Ricotta Hotcakes on page 128. They're equally good made with frozen raspberries and can provide a welcome reminder of summer on a dreary, cold, grey morning. Or serve a winter dried fruit compote with dollops of mascarpone mixed with milk to make a spoonable consistency, and flavoured with a dash of vanilla extract and a little sugar or honey.

And if you do want to serve more of a main course, there's nothing nicer – or simpler – to make than a fluffy cheese omelette. Try the Goats' Cheese Omelette with Wild Garlic and Chervil or some Buckwheat Galettes with Parma Ham and Emmental (both on page 101).

For a variety of brunch bagels, see the following page (and the picture above).

# SANDWICHES AND SNACKS

**You don't really need me to tell you how to make a cheese sandwich but there may be variations on the theme that might not have crossed your mind.**

First, it's worth tailoring your bread to your cheese (see page 67). In general, softer and sliced breads are better with harder cheeses, and crustier breads like baguettes and ciabatta with soft or semi-soft cheeses. (The more moist the filling, the drier the bread you need.)

### A SORT OF PAN-BAGNAT

Pan-bagnat is traditionally a loaf of bread stuffed with Niçoise-style salad, but the options are endless. Many shops now sell big, flat rustic loaves that you can slice horizontally and fill with grilled or roast vegetables, such as courgettes, aubergines, onions and peppers, scatter with basil leaves and top with slices of **Mozzarella**. Press down firmly, wrap tightly in foil and refrigerate for an hour, then cut into wedges or vertical slices.

### CLASSIC AMERICAN HERO SANDWICH

This is a great vehicle for cheese. Fill a sub or torpedo roll with slices of salami, ham and/or mortadella, then top with slices of mild Swiss cheese like **Emmental** and finely sliced sweet-pickled cucumber. Another deli-inspired classic would be to fill a freshly baked ciabatta with chargrilled steak and onions topped with melted **blue cheese**.

### SALAD ROLLS

Any combination of ingredients that makes a good salad tends to taste pretty good wedged between two slices of bread or in a roll. **Mozzarella**, tomatoes and basil, for instance,

(try making this with slow-roasted tomatoes for a change) or a chicken Caesar sandwich – sliced chicken breast, shaved **Parmesan**, shredded lettuce and Caesar dressing.

### CLASSIC SANDWICH FILLINGS

Other good, simple fillings include **Cheddar** with home-made apple or tomato chutney (great with a traditional white tin loaf); **blue cheese** with celery; and **cream cheese** with watercress (both the latter are good with brown bread); and a long slice of baguette with **Brie** and a dollop of cranberry sauce makes an excellent snack over Christmas. For toasted sandwiches, such as paninis, see page 69.

### A CHEESE AND BAGEL BRUNCH

Try this great – and easy to execute – idea for brunch (see picture on page 63). Serve three kinds of bagels: the traditional smoked salmon, **cream cheese** (mixed with finely chopped onion) and slices of sweet and sour cucumber; a wholewheat bagel filled with a mild, creamy blue cheese, such as **Dolcelatte**, fine slices of air-dried ham and sliced fresh figs; and cinnamon bagels filled with **cream cheese** mixed with chopped, candied pecan nuts or walnuts and fresh Medjool dates. (If you can't find candied nuts, warm pecans or walnuts in a non-stick frying pan with a little sugar and shake until the sugar has dissolved and coated the nuts.) Offer **Prosecco** or other sparkling wine, fresh orange juice and coffee.

CHEESE TIP

If you base your sandwich on more conventional fillings, such as ham and Swiss cheese, or smoked salmon and cream cheese, try putting it in a less conventional bread like a croissant or a bagel. For more bread suggestions, see page 67.

RIGHT *A pan-bagnat-style sandwich with courgettes, aubergines, onions, peppers, fresh basil and Mozzarella*

# CRACKERS AND CHEESE

Choosing a specific biscuit or cracker to go with your cheese, an idea pioneered by the innovative The Fine Cheese Co. in Bath, has really taken off in recent years and can turn a simple snack into a gourmet offering. Here are some combinations that work well.

◆ **Charcoal crackers** with young **goats' and sheep's cheeses** (it's the visual contrast of black against white as well as the taste that's so appealing)

◆ **Celery crackers** with **Stilton** and other creamy blue cheeses

◆ **Fennel-, caraway- or cumin-spiced crackers** with washed-rind cheese

*ABOVE (From left) flatbread and goats' cheese, digestives and Cheddar, charcoal crackers and Perroche, baguette and Brie, walnut and raisin bread and Stilton, ciabatta and Mozzarella*

◆ **Chive crackers** with **Brie**

◆ **Oatcakes** with rich, creamy cheeses (and smoked oatcakes with blue cheese and crispy bacon!)

◆ **Sweet wholemeal digestive biscuits** and **Cheddar**

◆ **Scandinavian-style crispbreads** with mild semi-soft cheeses like **Havarti**

◆ **Seeded, crisp flatbreads** with creamy **cows', goats' or sheep's cheeses**

◆ **Breadsticks** and **Mozzarella**

When you're choosing a cracker or biscuit, think about the texture as well as the flavour. Softer, spreadable cheeses need a firm base that won't crumble, while harder cheeses can be on a slightly more crumbly biscuit like an oatcake or a wholemeal digestive biscuit. (Not everyone likes sweet biscuits with cheese, so always offer a choice.) It's also impressive – and easy – to make your own, which you can do well in advance (see page 136).

# BREAD AND CHEESE

Isn't this the best ever combination – a simple pairing of artisanal ingredients that makes a perfect meal without the slightest effort? But there are so many cheeses – and so many breads. The most flexible type of bread in my view is a rustic country loaf, which could be an unbleached white, a mixture of flours or a sourdough. As a general rule, crusty bread like baguette works better with softer cheeses, while firmer breads seem a better complement to harder cheeses.

◆ **Baguette** with **Brie** and **Camembert**

◆ **Traditional white loaves** are the traditional choice for a Ploughman's. Good with **Cheddar**, **Double or Single Gloucester** and other hard British regional cheeses.

◆ **Sourdough bread** goes with all kinds of cheeses, particularly **washed-rind** and **hard sheep's cheeses**

◆ **Walnut bread or walnut and raisin breads** are flexible but particularly good with **blue cheeses** and **goats' cheeses**

◆ **Mixed grain breads** suit regional British cheeses, such as **Cheddar, Cheshire** and **Lancashire**

◆ **Rye bread** – light rye goes with Alpine cheeses like **Beaufort** and **Comté**; dark rye with creamy, spreadable cheeses

◆ **Rye breads with caraway or fennel seeds** (see page 132) work with **washed-rind** and **sheep's cheeses**

◆ **Spiced sweet breads** e.g. *pain d'épice* complement **Roquefort** and other strongly flavoured blues

◆ **Dense fruit breads** pair well with creamy blues, such as **Stilton**

◆ **Soft or crisp flatbreads and breadsticks** go with **soft goats' cheeses** and **labneh** (see page 140)

◆ **Olive or rosemary-flavoured breads** suit tangy sheep's cheeses like **Feta**

◆ **Ciabatta** and **Mozzarella** are made for each other

Introduce some variety into your bread basket by adding slices of grilled bread.

*Creamy blue cheese on walnut bread, grilled and topped with caramelized onions*

# CHEESE ON TOAST

**Some form of cheese and toasted bread is probably in all our culinary repertoires, whether it's a simple case of laying slices of cheese on a piece of toast and popping it under the grill or making a 'toastie' or a panini in an electric sandwich toaster or contact grill. Often it's a question of finding a use for some leftover cheese and less than fresh bread, but it can be a great deal more than that.**

If you're making cheese on toast for guests, try using a strong rather than a mild cheese for a change. Washed-rind cheeses, such as **Taleggio** and **Maroilles**, melt beautifully over a piece of grilled sourdough bread, for instance. (You can even rub a little raw garlic on the grilled surface of the bread if you're a garlic fan!) Creamy blue cheeses are great grilled or melted on toasted walnut bread – a good way of using up the remnants from a cheese board. You could add a layer of caramelized onions on top of the melted cheese to make a more substantial snack or a starter.

Try introducing other ingredients to your toasted sandwiches too to make them more interesting. Crispy bacon, fried apple slices and an Alpine cheese, such as **Beaufort**, for example, are delicious in a toasted ciabatta or panini roll, as are grilled vegetables with **Mozzarella** and grilled portobello mushrooms with **Taleggio**. (Almost anything you can put into a pizza you can put into a panini.)

# SOUP, CROSTINI AND CROUTONS

It's also useful to have a supply of crostini and croutons on hand to serve with soup. You can obviously make crostini with stale bread but I find them so useful that I tend to make batches with a fresh ciabatta loaf. Simply cut the bread on the diagonal into thin, even slices, spray or drizzle lightly with olive oil and bake in a preheated oven at 180°C (350°F) Gas 4 for 15 minutes until crisp. Leave to cool and store in an airtight container for up to 1 week. Topped with a light, moussey young goats' or sheep's cheese and a sprinkling of herbs they make an attractive alternative to bread for a fresh vegetable soup (I particularly like them with pea and broccoli soup).

For croutons, cut your bread into smaller pieces (unless you're making them for French Onion Soup on page 98) and bake them longer until they are hard, otherwise they'll go soggy when they hit the hot liquid or come into contact with melted cheese.

You could also serve miniature Welsh rarebits (grated Cheddar mixed with a little flour and English mustard powder, melted into a couple of spoonfuls of beer and seasoned with black pepper and a dash of Worcestershire sauce – see page 146 for regular-sized Welsh Rarebits). You can cut any kind of cheese toast into fingers – a nice accompaniment to winter vegetable soups, such as carrot, cauliflower, and pumpkin or butternut squash. With a stash of crostini and croutons and a hunk of cheese in your fridge, you'll always have the makings of a delicious snack.

# CHEESE ALFRESCO

**Just as wintertime has its own special cheese dishes (see Après-ski Cheese and Festive Cheese on pages 79 and 83 respectively), so some cheeses are perfectly suited to summer and outdoor eating.**

In general, it's the younger, fresher cheeses that suit summer best. Top of the list in my book are **goats' cheese** and **Feta** because they're so good with summer produce, particularly grilled vegetables such as peppers, courgettes and aubergines. A platter of vegetables topped with crumbled cheese, drizzled with oil and scattered with chopped fresh mint makes a perfect opener for a barbecue.

## GRILLED AND MELTED CHEESE

There are also cheeses you can actually grill. The most widely available one is the Greek and Cypriot cheese **Halloumi**, which keeps its shape even when exposed to an open fire. Marinate it in a little herb-infused oil, then either grill it in slices (a useful meat substitute for vegetarians) or cut it into cubes and thread it on skewers with vegetables such as courgettes, peppers and onions or simply with bay leaves, to create vegetarian kebabs. The Greek cheese **Kasseri** can be used in a similar way.

Other cheeses can be melted over grilled meat, such as burgers and steaks, to delicious effect, adding a slightly smoky taste to your favourite cheeseburger. **Taleggio** and milder **Gorgonzolas** (known as **Gorgonzola dolce** or **Dolcelatte**) are particularly good for this.

*LEFT Barbecued Halloumi and bay leaf kebabs*

## PICNIC CHEESE

If you're taking cheese on a picnic, it's better to avoid the more pungent types and keep it simple. A medium-matured, not-too-runny **Brie** with a baguette and a bagful of cherries is a lovely picnic treat. **Camembert** works well too, as does a good-quality cream cheese, which you can transport in its own pot (delicious with peaches and nectarines).

An alternative – and a good one – is to incorporate the cheese element of the meal in a finished dish, such as a quiche (e.g. the Leek and Blue Cheese Quiche with Hazelnut Pastry on page 115) or a flavoured bread of the type the French call 'cake' (e.g. the Quick Courgette, Feta and Mint Bread on page 132). Both are also good components of a casual alfresco supper. You can cut the 'cake' up into cubes and hand it round with drinks, as many French hostesses do.

Labneh with Herbs, Raw Vegetables and Flatbread on page 140 also makes a fresh and healthy grazing plate for an outdoor meal, as does a light cheese dip with a selection of raw vegetables.

## CHEESE-BASED SALADS

These make an easy and appealing warm-weather starter or, scaled up, attractive platters for a summer buffet. Try the Feta, Cucumber and Mint, and Heirloom Tomato, Burrata and Basil salads on page 94. Or for a simple family supper on the patio, try the delicious summery Courgette, Mint and Goats' Cheese Soup on page 98.

## CHEESE TIP

Pack it carefully! Cheese is a highly perishable food, so if you're taking it on a picnic you should obviously take care to transport it in a cool bag. Softer cheeses can easily squash and lose their shape so make sure they are well wrapped (preferably not in clingfilm, which can make them 'sweaty') or transported in a plastic box. And once you have unpacked it, keep it in the shade so that it remains cool and fresh. Personally, I wouldn't take a very smelly cheese on a picnic – it's amazing how its aroma can permeate a car, even from the boot!

# CHEESE AND WINE PARTIES

It must be at least 40 years ago now that cheese and wine parties were all the rage. You can see why – they were a simple way to entertain. No cooking, just a bit of cutting up. And the cheese was so bland that by and large there was never any problem serving red wine.

Maybe it's time to revisit these parties now that the range of cheeses open to us is greater, and of much higher quality than ever before. But let's update them and give them a stylish spin.

Over the next few pages you'll find a few ideas inspired by cheeses from other countries, but here are four suggestions that should impress your cheese-loving guests.

*Cheddar and Cracked Pepper Straws, and Champagne*

### CHEESE AND WINE 'STATIONS'

This is a great way to enjoy wine and cheese together and learn a little in the process. Set up four to six tables around the room, depending how much room you have, each with a different style of cheese and a different wine and some accompanying biscuits and/or bread. They could include:

◆ A **goats' cheese** with **Sauvignon Blanc** (it's always good to have at least a couple of cheeses for those who are intolerant to cows' milk)
◆ A **Brie-** or **Camembert-style** cheese with a fruity **Beaujolais** or **Pinot Noir**
◆ A **Cheddar** with an oaked **Chardonnay** and a **Merlot** (it will be interesting for your guests to see how the two compare)
◆ A **hard sheep's cheese** with a **Rioja** or other **Tempranillo-based red**
◆ A washed-rind cheese, such as **Munster** with a **Gewurztraminer**
◆ A **blue cheese** with **port** (for **Stilton**, for example, see the many other drink pairings on page 47). You could, of course, carry out a similar exercise with different beers and cheeses. Check out the recommended matches on page 42. Or surprise guests with an apple-flavoured drinks and cheese evening based on the pairings on pages 40–41.

### CHEESE AND CHAMPAGNE PARTY

Well, it doesn't have to be **Champagne** – a cheaper kind of fizz would be fine – but sparkling wine does go surprisingly well with cheese, particularly cheese pastries and biscuits.

You could lay on a range of different canapés, such as gougères (cheese-flavoured choux puffs); Cheddar and Cracked Pepper Straws (see page 136) or other little crisp cheese biscuits or tartlets made with cheese pastry; individual quiches (make miniature versions of the Leek and Blue Cheese Quiche with Hazelnut Pastry on page 115); mini cheese muffins (scale down the Double Cheese and Bacon Muffins on page 131); crostini topped with cheese; and mini-sandwiches or blinis topped with cream cheese and smoked salmon. (There is no reason why you should make all these yourself. You can buy excellent cheese biscuits these days, for example.)

### A CHEESE-THEMED DINNER PARTY

Your guests will be amazed at how different each course will taste. Kick off with one of the nibbles above, then you could serve the Parmesan Custards (see page 91) or one of the cheese salads on pages 94–95, steak with balsamic onions and molten blue cheese or roast lamb with Mushroom Dauphinois (see page 123) and the Lemon and Blueberry Upside-down Cheesecakes (see page 128), pairing each course with a matching wine – refer to the suggestions under individual recipes.

### A MAC 'N' CHEESE 'N' WINE SUPPER

Serve the two macaroni cheese recipes on page 120 and a choice of red and white wine. A fun and frugal evening!

See also the suggestions in Cutting Your Cheese Calories on page 153.

RIGHT *A cheese and wine station featuring Brie, glasses of Pinot Noir and baguettes*

# ROUND-THE-WORLD CHEESE

We tend to think of cheese as coming from the great cheese-producing nations of the world – France, Italy and Great Britain – but many other countries have a thriving cheese culture, such as Greece, Spain, Portugal, Mexico, the USA and Australia. Here are some simple ideas for internationally themed cheese events.

## CHEESE TAPAS

This is possibly one of the easiest themes to organize since tapas ingredients are so widely available these days. A very simple get-together for a drink could involve some fine slices of **Manchego** with membrillo (quince paste), sliced chorizo, Marcona almonds and green olives with glasses of fresh **manzanilla sherry** (see picture opposite).

For a more substantial meal, you could add the Red Pepper and Manchego Tortilla on page 102, red peppers stuffed with goats' cheese or some *croquetas* (crisp little deep-fried rissoles with a creamy, cheesy filling). There are also other interesting Spanish cheeses to explore, including **Majorero** from the Canary Islands, and two powerful blues, **Valdeón** and **Cabrales**, which you could pair with sweet sherry and raisins.

## CHEESE SMØRREBRØD

Cheese is not the central component of the traditional Danish and Norwegian smørrebrød table but makes an enjoyable addition to the usual fish- and meat-based offerings. Use your imagination (and the ideas on page 64) to create open sandwiches using Scandinavian cheeses, such as **Jarlsberg**, **Havarti**, **Samso** and **Danish Blue**. You could try **cream cheese** topped with smoked salmon and cod roe, a slice of **Samso** topped with smoked beef or ham, finely sliced raw onions and pickled cucumber, and **Danish Blue** with figs.

Alternatively, lay out a selection of platters of different meats, cheeses and salads for a traditional Swedish-style smorgasbord (which is essentially a buffet-style table of savoury dishes). Miniaturized versions of the cheese and cucumber verrines on page 88 would fit in particularly well with this. **Beer** and **aquavit** are traditional accompaniments.

## CHEESE ANTIPASTI

Again, this is a very simple way of entertaining at short notice. A selection of preserved grilled vegetables, such as artichokes, mushrooms and peppers, with Parma or San Daniele ham, **Mozzarella** balls, ciabatta and breadsticks makes a delicious, impromptu feast (see picture on page 77). Serve with a crisp, dry Italian white, such as **Pinot Grigio** from the Alto Adige, a **Prosecco** or a lightly chilled **Valpolicella**.

If you wanted to add a couple of hot dishes, you could serve some *arancini* (deep-fried risotto balls) and *pizzette* (mini-pizzas) or, of course, go on to a pasta course.

LEFT *Classic tapas: Manchego with membrillo (quince paste), chorizo, Marcona almonds, green olives and manzanilla sherry*

### BEER AND BURRITOS

Beer and burritos is a great idea for a Mexican-themed evening. All you have to do is provide the ingredients for the burritos (see the recipe on page 109 for guidance) and let people make their own. As well as the ubiquitous **Sol**, there are some good Mexican beers around in specialist shops, such as **Negra Modelo**, a dark, flavoursome beer.

For a shorter, more impromptu get-together, serve **margaritas** and *quesadillas* – little pan-fried cheese sandwiches made with tortillas. You can vary the filling by making them with ham, refried beans (see page 109) or simply with chopped jalapeño peppers. Cheese *empanadas* (mini-pasties), which are popular throughout Central and South America, are also delicious but slightly more time-consuming to make.

### CHEESE MEZZE OR MEZEDES

Serve home-made Labneh (see page 140) with fresh herbs, dukkah and flatbread or with raw vegetables, such as carrots, cucumber and celery, olives and pickled chillies for a light, Middle Eastern-inspired meal. Wine wouldn't be traditional with this kind of food; you could serve **beer** and **raki** (or **ouzo**) but might also want to offer a soft drink like **pomegranate juice**.

The Greeks have a similar tradition of small plates called 'mezedes', which might include preserved **Feta** or deep-fried or grilled **Kasseri** or **Kefalotyri** cheese served with a squeeze of lemon. You could add some taramasalata, grilled or preserved octopus, stuffed vine leaves or *gigantes*, the tasty butter beans in tomato sauce. If you wanted a more substantial course, add some wedges of *spanakopita*, Greece's famous spinach and Feta pie. Again, **ouzo** or **beer** would be traditional accompaniments but there are such good Greek wines around now that it would be a shame not to try one. I'd serve a crisp **Assyrtiko**.

### A LATE-NIGHT FRENCH BISTRO SUPPER

Follow the example of Parisian party-goers who used to go to Les Halles in the early hours of the morning for sustaining bowlfuls of onion soup, topped with slices of grilled country bread and melted cheese (see recipe on page 98). It's a great finale to an evening at the theatre or a chilly outdoor sporting event. A simple dry white wine (**Aligoté** is traditional), some crusty bread and a leafy green salad make perfect accompaniments. Finish the meal off with a classic French fruit tart. (See also Après-ski Cheese overleaf.)

RIGHT *Cheese antipasti: Mozzarella balls with preserved grilled artichokes, mushrooms and peppers, Parma ham and breadsticks*

# APRES-SKI CHEESE

**Even if you don't go skiing, you can't fail to be captivated by the traditional après-ski hot cheese dishes that are served up after a day on the slopes. I can't think of better dishes to welcome friends round on a cold winter evening than deliciously, meltingly gooey fondue, raclette and tartiflette.**

With all of these melted cheese dishes, it pays to use the best, authentic ingredients. **Fondue** is probably the best known – and the hardest to get right until you've made it a couple of times (a bit like learning to swim or ride a bicycle!) You can find a recipe on page 106 (made with cider, which works just as well as white wine) but the key points to bear in mind are: make sure your cheese (usually **Gruyère** and **Emmental**) is at room temperature; take the pan off the heat before you start adding the cheese; and stir with a figure-of-eight rather than a circular motion, which can cause the cheese to ball up and separate from the liquid. In order to keep control of the process, it's best to make it for a small group – no more than six – unless you have a couple of fondue sets and an extra pair of hands to supervise the second batch.

**Raclette**, which is of Swiss origin and the name of both the cheese and the dish, is better for a larger group. You can buy or hire a purpose-made raclette maker, which may either consist of a number of small pans or a more complicated grill-like mechanism into which you wedge the cheese, pass it directly under the heat and shear the molten cheese off into a dish of boiled new potatoes garnished with pearl onions and gherkins. You can also offer some air-dried country ham and sliced vegetables, such as courgettes and peppers, to eat with the molten cheese.

**Tartiflette** (see recipe on page 112), which comes from the Savoie region of France, is probably the most straightforward of the three dishes. It's a wickedly rich bake of potatoes, onions, bacon and **Reblochon** cheese quite similar in style to a gratin dauphinois. It makes a great winter supper dish with a green salad.

You could also incorporate an 'après-ski' element to your winter entertaining by serving a **Vacherin**, one of my all-time favourite cheeses. It goes by different names depending on which side of the Alps it's made – France or Switzerland – but is generally marketed as **Vacherin Mont d'Or** or **Vacherin du Haut-Doubs** (see page 18). It comes in a box and looks a bit like a giant Camembert with an undulating pinkish rind but it has a wonderfully unctuous creamy interior. You can either serve it at room temperature or bake it in its box for a fondue-like effect. Again, new potatoes (sprinkled with crunchy sea salt) are an excellent accompaniment.

Note that red wine tends to be positively unpleasant with all these dishes. A **crisp, fruity dry white** is infinitely preferable, or even, in the case of **Vacherin**, a glass of **Champagne**.

**LEFT** *Baked Vacherin Mont d'Or with boiled new potatoes and sea salt*

# FESTIVE CHEESE

**The time of year when we all want to put on a particularly spectacular cheese offering is the Christmas and Thanksgiving holiday period. And that's as much about dressing up your board and the other ingredients you pick as the cheeses you choose.**

I like to create a colourful cheese board full of warm, rich colours by mixing the traditional accompaniments of satsumas, clementines and nuts with some of the fabulous products you can now buy in any supermarket or deli: big lush raisins, fresh Medjool dates (instead of the oversweet, sticky preserved ones of my youth), slices of delicious Spanish fig roll, a few candied pecan nuts, even some pieces of brilliant orange dried mango or a rosy pomegranate all look fabulously festive.

Blue cheese is, of course, traditional for Christmas but it could just as well be a rich **Shropshire Blue** as a **Stilton**. Partner it with a fine, golden English **Cheddar**, a brilliant orange-rinded cheese, such as a **Stinking Bishop** or French **Epoisses**, and a deep orange **Mimolette** from Northern France and you've echoed those rich colours in your cheese board too – almost like a classic Dutch still life.

You can also create pretty seasonal cheese plates with these ingredients – hunt around for gold plates (often to be found in cheap chain or party stores).

## OTHER IDEAS FOR THANKSGIVING AND CHRISTMAS

◆ For a Christmas twist on a classic cream tea, bake a batch of scones and fill them with **cream cheese** and cranberry sauce instead of cream and jam. You could also offer some **Parmesan** scones or mini cheese muffins studded with dried cranberries.

◆ For a quick snack, halve baguettes lengthways and fill with sliced **Brie** and cranberry sauce or use the same ingredients to top crostini for a quick and easy canapé. (Leftover holiday cheese can also be whizzed into a tasty cheese spread for crostini toppings – see page 146.)

◆ For those who are sated with sweet things, finish a meal with a scoop or two of **Stilton** with some toasted walnut bread, some jewel-red Spiced Quince Compote with Red Wine and Cloves (see page 145) and a glass of **port**

◆ For a show-stopping 'cheesert', take a small whole **Brie**, carefully slice the rind off the top and spread with a thick cranberry, raspberry and cherry compote. Serve it in wedges, like a cheesecake.

◆ Make Christmas **mascarpone** 'trifles' similar to the Lemon and Blueberry Upside-down Cheesecakes on page 128: start with a compote like the one above – laced with a dash of **cherry brandy** if you have some – a vanilla-flavoured mascarpone topping and a scattering of caramelized pine nuts

## HALLOWE'EN CHEESE

Hallowe'en is becoming such a major celebration in its own right that it deserves its own cheese board. It would have to be largely orange, as there aren't any black cheeses I'm aware of, although you could serve an **ash-coated goats' cheese** or a **black wax-coated Cheddar** and have some

ready-to-eat prunes and charcoal biscuits on the side. (Hallowe'en is nothing if not kitsch!) Perfect candidates for orange cheeses would be **Mimolette**, as described above, a washed-rind cheese, such as **Epoisses** or **Stinking Bishop** (the idea of a stinky cheese seems particularly suitable for Hallowe'en, I feel) and **Red Leicester** from England. You could even carry the black – or near black – and orange theme through to the drinks. **Port** and **elderberry wine** are pretty dark in colour or try a **pumpkin ale**.

### CHEESE TIP

Although nuts in general are a good partner for cheese, there are specific pairings that stand out, for example walnuts and pecan nuts (candied or uncoated) with blue cheeses, such as Gorgonzola or Cashel Blue; almonds with sheep's cheeses, such as Manchego; Brazil nuts with cream cheese; and hazelnuts with goats' cheese.

LEFT *Mimolette with Medjool dates, dried figs, nuts and tawny port*
PAGES 80–81 *Shropshire Blue, Mimolette, Epoisses, clementines, raisins, fresh Medjool dates, slices of Spanish fig roll, fresh pomegranate and port*

COOKING
WITH CHEESE

# COOKING WITH CHEESE

**Most of us, I suspect, get stuck in a rut when it comes to using cheese in cooking. If we need a hard grating cheese, it's Parmesan; for a fondue, Gruyère; for a sauce, Cheddar; for a salad, a goats' cheese or a crumbly blue. But there are, as I hope you'll discover over the next few pages, many other possibilities.**

The main thing to get out of your mind when cooking with cheese is that it's somehow 'a waste' to use a good cheese for cooking, in much the same way that people think they shouldn't use a decent wine. No one would think that about meat or fish. You get out of a dish what you put into it in terms of quality. Moreover, using stronger, more intensely flavoured cheeses means you can use less of them, which makes for healthier recipes (see page 153) and a lighter-textured dish.

Of course cheese is an expensive ingredient and you wouldn't necessarily want to cook with a rare and special cheese you've bought to savour in its own right. But it's surprising the effect you can achieve by using top-quality cheese on a pizza (see page 111) or a washed-rind cheese, such as **Reblochon** or **Taleggio** (one of my favourite cooking cheeses), in a tart. And it's a valuable way of using up the last remnants of a fine cheese that might otherwise go to waste.

There may also be uses for cheeses you might not have thought of. Baking a whole **Camembert**, for example, is an easy way of producing an instant fondue. Lightly flour slices of **Mozzarella di bufala** and fry them for quick, delicious cheese fritters. Marinate **Halloumi** with olive oil and herbs and grill it on the barbecue. Make crisp little cheese crisps from grated Cheddar (see page 120) and use them to make the ultimate Extra-crispy Macaroni Cheese

(also on page 120). Mix **mascarpone** with lemon curd for an instant and creamily indulgent dessert (see page 128). Even making your own cheese is child's play, as you'll see if you try the easy recipe for the delicious Middle Eastern cheese labneh (see page 140).

You'll get the best results from the cheese you use if you follow a few general guidelines. In general, it's better to cut off the rind, certainly on well-matured, hard cheeses, such as **Cheddar**, although there are exceptions, such as in Tartiflette (see page 112) where the rind of the **Reblochon** really contributes to the flavour of the finished dish.

If you are grating cheese or trying to shave fine slices, it's easier to do this with cheese that's just been taken out of the fridge, although for some recipes, such as fondue (see page 106), you will need to bring the cheese to room temperature before using it. And, with the exception of fondue, don't cook cheese too long over a direct heat or it can develop a stringy texture. Cheese is best added to a sauce once it's been taken off the heat.

## CHEESES FOR MELTING

Gruyère, Emmental, Fontina, Lancashire

## CHEESES FOR GRATINS

Parmesan, Grana Padano, Pecorino

## CHEESES FOR PIZZA

Mozzarella, Taleggio, Gorgonzola (if you fancy a blue)

## CHEESES FOR SALADS

Young **goats' cheeses**, crumbly white cheeses, such as **Caerphilly**, crumbly blues, such as **Stilton**. Shaveable cheeses, such as **Parmesan** and **Pecorino** also work well.

## CHEESES FOR DESSERTS

Ricotta, mascarpone

# CHEESE AND CUCUMBER VERRINES

**'Verrines' are all the rage in France – stylish little starters or puddings that are layered in a glass. Here are two variations on a theme, based on the very complementary ingredients of cucumber and soft cheese. The two verrines look fantastic together at a summer supper party or buffet. Serve a crisp, dry German Riesling or Austrian Grüner Veltliner with both.**

## CUCUMBER AND RICOTTA VERRINES WITH PRAWNS

2 cucumbers, peeled

3 small sheets of leaf gelatine

50 ml semi-skimmed milk

250 g ricotta

150 ml low-fat yoghurt

2 tablespoons finely chopped fresh dill leaves, plus several sprigs to garnish

2 teaspoons strained lemon juice, plus extra lemon juice to season the prawns

150 g cooked, peeled prawns

sea salt and white pepper

*6–8 tumblers or small glass dishes*

**SERVES 6–8**

Cut the cucumbers in half lengthways and scoop out the seeds with the tip of a teaspoon. Halve lengthways again, then cut each piece into 3 long strips and cut across into small dice. Put in a colander and sprinkle with salt. Leave for about 20 minutes.

Put the gelatine sheets in a shallow dish and sprinkle over 3 tablespoons cold water. Leave to soak for 5 minutes. Meanwhile, gently heat the milk in a small saucepan until almost boiling. When the gelatine is soft, remove each sheet from the water and drop them into the warm milk. Remove from the heat and stir until the gelatine has dissolved.

Put the ricotta and yoghurt in a food processor and whizz until smooth. Tip into a bowl, scraping the food processor bowl thoroughly with a rubber spatula. Stir in the milk and gelatine, the dill and lemon juice. Rinse the cucumber with cold water and pat dry. Fold just over half the cucumber into the ricotta mixture and season with salt to taste. Divide the mixture between the tumblers, cover and refrigerate for 2 hours to set. Cover the remaining cucumber and refrigerate too.

Scatter the creams with the remaining cucumber and top with prawns. Squeeze over a little lemon juice and decorate with dill.

## CUCUMBER AND FROMAGE FRAIS VERRINES WITH SMOKED SALMON

3 small sheets of leaf gelatine

300 ml light vegetable stock (use ⅓ vegetable stock cube or 1 teaspoon vegetable bouillon powder)

freshly squeezed juice of 1 lime

1 teaspoon sugar

2 medium/large cucumbers, peeled

3 tablespoons finely snipped fresh chives, plus extra to garnish

200 g fromage frais

2–3 tablespoons semi-skimmed milk

125 g wafer-thin smoked salmon, cut into strips

sea salt and white pepper

*6–8 tumblers or small glass dishes*

**SERVES 6–8**

Put the gelatine sheets in a shallow dish and sprinkle over 3 tablespoons cold water. Leave to soak for 5 minutes.

Pour the vegetable stock into a small saucepan with the lime juice and sugar and heat until almost boiling. When the gelatine is soft, remove each sheet from the water and drop them into the pan. Remove from the heat and stir until the gelatine has dissolved, then strain into a jug and set aside to cool.

Cut the cucumbers in half lengthways and scoop out the seeds with the tip of a teaspoon. Halve lengthways again, then cut each piece into 3 long strips and cut across into small dice. Put in a colander and sprinkle with salt. Leave for about 20 minutes, then rinse with cold water and pat dry. Mix with the chives. Half-fill the tumblers with the cucumber and pour over enough cooled stock to cover. Cover and refrigerate for at least 1½ hours to set.

When the jelly is firm, mix the fromage frais with enough milk to make a soft, spoonable consistency, season and spoon a layer over the jelly. Top with smoked salmon and decorate with chives.

# PARMESAN CUSTARDS WITH ANCHOVY TOASTS

A delectable starter that has probably been one of the most popular recipes of the past year since Rowley Leigh added it to the menu of his London restaurant, Le Café Anglais. I keep meaning to order something different but never manage to.

300 ml single cream
300 ml whole milk
100 g Parmesan, finely grated
4 egg yolks
cayenne pepper
12 anchovy fillets
50 g unsalted butter
8 very thin slices of pain de campagne
sea salt and finely ground white pepper

*8 x 80-ml ramekins or ovenproof dishes, buttered*

**SERVES 8**

Mix the cream, milk and all but 1 tablespoon of the Parmesan in a heatproof bowl, place it over a saucepan of boiling water and warm it gently until the Parmesan has melted. Remove the bowl from on top of the pan and leave to cool completely.

Preheat the oven to 150°C (300°F) Gas 2.

Whisk the egg yolks, a pinch of salt, a pinch of white pepper and a little cayenne pepper into the cool cream mixture, then pour into the prepared ramekins. Place the ramekins in an ovenproof dish in the oven, then pour boiling water from the kettle into the dish to reach halfway up the ramekins. Cover the whole dish with a sheet of buttered greaseproof paper and bake in the preheated oven for 15 minutes or until the custards have just set. Remove from the oven and turn on the grill.

Mash the anchovies and butter to make a smooth paste and spread over 4 of the slices of bread. Cover with the remaining bread and toast in a sandwich maker or panini machine. Sprinkle the remaining Parmesan over the warm custards and brown gently under the hot grill. Cut the toasted anchovy sandwiches into fingers and serve alongside the custards.

**What to drink:** Champagne is a great pairing with Parmesan but you could serve any similar dry sparkling wine.

*LEFT Parmesan Custards with Anchovy Toasts*

# ICEBERG LETTUCE WEDGES WITH BLUE CHEESE DRESSING

This is a great side dish for a burger or steak. Don't be tempted to whizz the dressing ingredients together otherwise it will turn an ugly greyish-green.

1 small/medium iceberg lettuce

**DRESSING**
2 tablespoons white wine vinegar or cider vinegar
30 ml extra virgin olive oil
75 ml grapeseed oil
2 tablespoons double or whipping cream
50 g crumbly blue cheese, e.g. Stilton or Fourme d'Ambert
3 spring onions, trimmed and very finely chopped
freshly squeezed lemon juice, to taste
sea salt and freshly ground black pepper

**SERVES 4**

First make the dressing. Whisk the vinegar with a little salt and pepper, then gradually whisk in the 2 oils. Finally, whisk in the cream. Roughly break up the blue cheese and add to the dressing, together with most of the spring onions, leaving a little for garnish. Set the mixture aside for 15–30 minutes to allow the flavours to amalgamate.

Remove any soft or damaged outer leaves from the lettuce, cut off the base, then cut the lettuce into 4 wedges. Soak in iced water for 10 minutes, then remove, shake off any excess water and dry thoroughly with kitchen paper or a clean tea towel.

Taste the dressing again, adding more salt and pepper if you think it needs it, and a squeeze of lemon juice. Put a lettuce wedge on each plate, spoon over the dressing and sprinkle with the remaining spring onions.

**Variation:** You could use the same dressing with halved or quartered Little Gem lettuces. It also works well with a spinach and raw mushroom salad.

**What to drink:** A white Burgundy or similar Chardonnay would be great with this.

THIS PAGE *Feta, Cucumber and Mint Spring Salad*
RIGHT *Heirloom Tomato, Burrata and Basil Summer Salad*

# SEASONAL CHEESE SALADS

The perfect basis for a light lunch that can be varied from season to season

## FETA, CUCUMBER AND MINT SPRING SALAD

A fabulously fresh-tasting summery salad that I discovered in one of my favourite London restaurants, Ransome's Dock, which in turn adapted it from a dish at Zuni Café in San Francisco!

2 mini-cucumbers
6 breakfast radishes
2 good handfuls of rocket
a small handful of fresh mint leaves
150 g Feta, broken into small pieces
10–15 small black olives

**DRESSING**
3 tablespoons extra virgin olive oil
1 tablespoon red wine vinegar
a good squeeze of lemon juice
sea salt and freshly ground black pepper

**SERVES 2**

To make the dressing, whisk or shake the ingredients together in a lidded jar.

Cut the cucumbers in half lengthways and scoop out the seeds with the tip of a teaspoon. Slice lengthways using a mandoline or vegetable peeler to make wafer-thin slices. Trim the radishes and thinly slice on the diagonal.

Put the rocket, mint, cucumber and radishes in a bowl and toss together with the dressing. Add the crumbled Feta and toss lightly again, then scatter over the olives. Divide the ingredients between 2 plates, piling them up in a mound. Serve with ciabatta or other crusty bread.

**What to drink:** A crisp, fruity white or a dry rosé.

## HEIRLOOM TOMATO, BURRATA AND BASIL SUMMER SALAD

A deluxe version of the eternally popular tomato and Mozzarella salad using Burrata, a wonderful fresh cheese from Puglia which is based on Mozzarella and cream. A real high summer treat.

400 g mixed heirloom tomatoes in different colours
3–4 tablespoons fragrant, grassy extra virgin olive oil, plus extra to drizzle
300 g Burrata
leaves from 3 sprigs of fresh basil (purple basil, if possible)
balsamic vinegar, to drizzle
sea salt and freshly ground black pepper

**SERVES 4**

Remove the stalks from the tomatoes. Slice the larger ones and halve the smaller ones or leave them whole. Transfer to a bowl. Spoon over the olive oil, season with salt and pepper, toss together and leave for 10 minutes.

Divide the tomatoes between 4 small plates. Roughly tear the Burrata into small chunks and distribute them over the tomatoes. Scatter with the basil leaves. Drizzle over a little more oil and some balsamic vinegar, and serve with crusty bread.

**What to drink:** A lightly oaked Sauvignon or a Sauvignon-Sémillon blend.

# COMTE, APPLE AND HAZELNUT AUTUMN SALAD

A pretty autumnal salad that is substantial enough to serve as a main course.

25 g shelled hazelnuts

1 tablespoon sunflower oil

100 g smoked bacon lardons
or pancetta cubes

1 Little Gem lettuce, leaves separated

75 g smoked chicken, torn into strips

60 g Comté or Beaufort (rind removed),
thinly sliced on the diagonal

1 Cox or Blenheim Orange apple,
quartered, cored and cut into wedges

a few root vegetable crisps

a small handful of fresh chives, snipped

## DRESSING

2 tablespoons crab apple jelly, rowan jelly
or redcurrant jelly

2 tablespoons pure apple juice

1 teaspoon cider vinegar

sea salt and freshly ground black pepper

## SERVES 2

Preheat the oven to 180°C (350°F) Gas 4.

Put the hazelnuts on a baking tray and roast in the preheated oven for 10 minutes, or until the skins turn dark brown. Leave to cool for a few minutes, then tip them onto a clean tea towel and rub off the skins. Cut the hazelnuts in half.

Heat the oil in a frying pan and fry the bacon until crisp. Take the pan off the heat, remove the bacon from the pan with a slotted spoon and transfer to a plate lined with kitchen paper. Pour off all but 1 tablespoon of the fat, add the crab apple jelly for the dressing and stir until melted, putting the pan back on the heat if necessary. Add the apple juice and cider vinegar and a splash of water if needed to thin the dressing. Season with salt and pepper and set aside.

Take 2 plates and arrange the lettuce leaves on each plate. Top with the bacon and smoked chicken, then the cheese and apple. Drizzle over the dressing and scatter with the hazelnuts, a few root vegetable crisps and the chives. Serve the remaining root vegetable crisps in a bowl alongside or offer some crusty bread.

**What to drink:** A glass of cider or lightly oaked Chenin Blanc or Chardonnay. A fruity red, such as a Pinot Noir, would work too.

# STICHELTON AND STEAK WINTER SALAD WITH ONIONS AND ROCKET

Stichelton is a wonderful new unpasteurized blue which is made to a similar recipe to Stilton (which you can easily substitute). A very easy and stylish supper for two.

250 g lean steak, trimmed of any fat

extra virgin olive oil

1 onion, thinly sliced

about 1 tablespoon balsamic vinegar

75 g cherry tomatoes

55 g rocket

60 g Stichelton or Stilton, rind removed

sea salt and freshly ground black pepper

## SERVES 2

Lay the steak on a sheet of greaseproof paper on a chopping board, cover with another sheet of greaseproof paper and beat out with a meat mallet or rolling pin. Rub a little olive oil into both sides of the steak and season lightly with salt and pepper. Heat a ridged griddle pan until almost smoking, then lay the steak in the pan and cook for 1 minute. Turn and cook for 1 minute on the other side, then transfer from the pan to a plate.

Turn down the heat under the pan slightly, smear a little oil over the onion slices and place them in a single layer in the pan. Cook for a couple of minutes until beginning to turn dark brown, then carefully turn and cook the other side. Set aside on another plate and drizzle over a little of the balsamic vinegar.

Finally, tip the cherry tomatoes into the pan with a little extra oil, if necessary, and roll them around until the skins begin to burst.

Cut the steak into fine slices with a sharp knife. Divide the rocket between 2 plates, top with the onions and arrange the tomatoes round the plate. Scatter over the steak slices and crumble over the Stichelton. Trickle over a little extra oil and balsamic vinegar and season with pepper. This salad is good with a crusty baguette, warm ciabatta or a baked potato.

**What to drink:** You might be surprised, given that red wine and blue cheese aren't generally the most accommodating of partners, but a fruity Cabernet Sauvignon will go well with this. (The steak and onions counteract the slight bitterness of the cheese.)

THIS PAGE *Cheese, Apple and Hazelnut Autumn Salad*
RIGHT *Stichelton and Steak Winter Salad with Onions and Rocket*

# COURGETTE, MINT AND GOATS' CHEESE SOUP

Cheese can be used both to add richness and texture to a soup, and also as a flavoursome topping. This deliciously light, summery soup combines both uses. You could vary the recipe by including broccoli or even peas, or substituting dill for the mint.

3 tablespoons olive oil

a small bunch of spring onions, trimmed and sliced

1 small/medium potato, thinly sliced

500 g small/medium courgettes

2 sprigs of fresh mint

750 ml vegetable stock (use a vegetable stock cube or 1 tablespoon vegetable bouillon powder)

25 g butter

125 g young, crumbly goats' cheese

sea salt and freshly ground black pepper

**SERVES 4**

Heat the oil in a heavy saucepan, then add the spring onions and potato. Stir, cover with a lid, reduce the heat and cook over low heat for about 7–8 minutes or until the potato starts to soften. Slice 1 of the courgettes and add to the pan along with the mint stalks (chop the leaves finely and set aside). Stir and cook for 1–2 minutes, then add 500 ml of the stock. Bring to the boil, then simmer until the potatoes are cooked (about 15–20 minutes). Meanwhile, grate the remaining courgettes and drain them in a colander, pressing them gently to extract any liquid.

Heat a large frying pan and add the butter. When the butter stops foaming, tip in the grated courgette and stir-fry for about 1 minute. Add the chopped mint leaves, fry for another 30 seconds, then set aside. Once the potatoes are tender, take the soup off the heat, remove the mint stalks and tip in three-quarters of the grated courgette mixture. Whizz the soup in batches in a food processor, returning the liquidized soup to a clean pan. Pour the remaining stock into the food processor to collect the remnants of the vegetable purée and pour into the soup. Reheat the soup to boiling point and take off the heat. Crumble in just under half the goats' cheese and whisk to amalgamate. Season to taste.

Quickly reheat the remaining grated courgette mixture. Ladle the soup into warm bowls, scatter a little grated courgette over the top and crumble over the remaining goats' cheese.

**What to drink:** Sauvignon Blanc or apple juice.

# FRENCH ONION SOUP

French onion soup is one of the classic bistro dishes, made luxuriant by its cheese and bread topping. Like many simple recipes it needs good ingredients. The critical thing to remember is to cook the onions long enough and to use a substantial, densely textured bread, preferably a couple of days old.

1 sourdough baguette or other long rustic loaf

2 tablespoons olive oil

50 g butter

2–3 large mild onions (about 700 g in total), thinly sliced

½ teaspoon sugar

½ teaspoon dried thyme

a glass of dry white wine (about 150 ml)

1.25 litres beef, chicken or vegetable stock (2 organic stock cubes)

white wine vinegar, to taste (optional)

125 g Gruyère (rind removed), coarsely grated

sea salt and freshly ground black pepper

**SERVES 4**

Preheat the oven to 180°C (350°F) Gas 4. Cut the bread into slices about 2 cm thick and lay on a baking tray. Bake in the preheated oven for 15–20 minutes or until crisp and lightly browned, then set aside. (You can do this ahead when you have the oven on.)

Heat the oil in a large ovenproof casserole, add the butter and tip in the onions. Stir so that they're thoroughly coated with oil and cook over low/medium heat, stirring them occasionally, until they go a rich, deep brown. This may take up to 40 minutes, depending on your onions. Add the sugar, if using, once they start to brown, and stir more regularly – you don't want to burn them. Once the onions are a good colour, stir in the thyme and wine and leave it to bubble up and reduce by half. Add the stock, bring back to the boil and simmer for about 20–25 minutes. Check for seasoning, adding salt and pepper to taste and a few drops of vinegar if you think it tastes too sweet. Preheat the grill.

Ladle the soup into 4 individual ovenproof bowls. Lay the slices of bread over the surface of the soup, pressing them down lightly. Scatter over the Gruyère and grill for 5–10 minutes until bubbling.

**What to drink:** Traditionally, the French would drink a crisp, dry white like an Aligoté with this kind of dish.

RIGHT *French Onion Soup*

# GOATS' CHEESE OMELETTE WITH WILD GARLIC AND CHERVIL

This is a recipe prompted by a spring visit to the farmers' market. If you haven't had goats' cheese in an omelette before, do try it – it has a surprising affinity with eggs.

a small handful of fresh chervil or parsley
2 large or 3 medium eggs
2 wild garlic leaves, finely shredded,
or some finely snipped fresh chives
15 g butter
40 g goats' cheese, crumbled
sea salt and freshly ground black pepper

**SERVES 1**

Pick over the chervil, cutting away the tougher stems, and chop finely. Beat the eggs in a bowl with a splash of water (about 1 tablespoon), add the chopped chervil and wild garlic leaves and beat again. Season lightly with salt and pepper.

Heat a medium-sized frying pan or omelette pan until hot, add the butter, swirl it round and pour in the beaten eggs and herbs, swirling them around the pan. Lift the edge of the omelette as it begins to cook, letting the liquid egg run from the centre to the edge. Scatter over the goats' cheese and leave for a minute to allow the omelette to brown. Add more pepper if you like. Fold one side of the omelette over and tip it onto a plate. You could serve this with some lightly dressed mixed salad leaves.

**What to drink:** A glass of smooth, dry white wine, such as an Alsace Pinot Blanc or an unoaked Chardonnay would pair well with this.

# BUCKWHEAT GALETTES WITH PARMA HAM AND EMMENTAL

These are based on the delicious dark buckwheat flour crêpes you find in Brittany and crêperies all over France, but they have been given a bit of an Italian twist with the inclusion of Parma ham and olive oil.

60 g buckwheat flour
60 g plain flour
½ teaspoon salt
2 large eggs
4 tablespoons olive oil
50 g butter
12 thin slices of Parma ham or other air-dried ham
150 g Emmental, grated
freshly ground black pepper

**MAKES 6–8 LARGE PANCAKES**

Put the 2 flours, the salt, eggs and half the oil in a food processor with 150 ml water. Whizz until smooth, then gradually add another 150 ml water so that you have a thin batter. Process for another minute, then leave to rest for 10 minutes. Alternatively, you can make the batter by hand with a whisk and a large bowl.

Gently melt 10 g of the butter with the remaining oil in a small saucepan and set aside. Heat a pancake pan or frying pan until moderately hot but not smoking. Pour in a little of the melted butter and oil and spread over the pan with kitchen paper. Pour in the batter with a ladle, tipping the pan as you do so, so that the batter runs quickly and evenly over the surface. Cook for about 30 seconds until no uncooked mixture shows, then flip the pancake over and cook for a further 30 seconds. Slip the pancake onto a warm plate and make the next pancake, greasing the pan as you go.

Once you've made all the pancakes, place 2–3 pieces of ham on each one and sprinkle with a small handful of Emmental, season with pepper and fold in half like a sandwich. Melt the remaining butter and pour a little into the pancake pan or frying pan. Wipe with kitchen paper. Heat the pancakes up 2 at a time, cooking on each side until they are crisp and the cheese has melted. Repeat with the remaining pancakes, greasing the pan between each batch, and serve straightaway with a green salad.

**What to drink:** A sparkling Normandy cider or still British cider would be delicious, or try a simple Vin Blanc.

*LEFT Goats' Cheese Omelette with Wild Garlic and Chervil*

# RED PEPPER AND MANCHEGO TORTILLA

The addition of cheese to a tortilla makes it substantial enough for a main course, as well as a stylish tapas dish. You may feel it's time-consuming to fry the vegetables separately but I find that it enormously improves the flavour and texture of the finished dish.

6 tablespoons Spanish extra virgin olive oil, plus extra to fry

1 large Spanish onion (about 250 g), very thinly sliced

1 large, flavoursome red pepper, quartered, deseeded and finely sliced (try to find outdoor-grown peppers if possible; you can also use a couple of marinated roasted peppers, in which case add them at the same time as the Manchego)

350 g salad potatoes, e.g. Charlotte, very thinly sliced

8 eggs

75 g Manchego, thinly sliced

sea salt and freshly ground black pepper

*a deep 23–24-cm frying pan*

**SERVES 4–6**

Heat 4 tablespoons of the oil in a large, deep lidded frying pan or wok, then fry the onion and pepper over medium heat until soft and beginning to brown at the edges. Remove from the pan with a slotted spoon, leaving behind the oil.

Add the remaining oil to the pan, heat for 1 minute, then tip in the potatoes and stir with a spatula to ensure the slices are separate and well coated in oil. Fry, stirring, for about 5–6 minutes until they start to brown, then reduce the heat, cover with the lid and cook for another 10–15 minutes until the potatoes are tender, turning them every so often so that they don't catch.

Tip the onion and pepper back into the pan, mix with the potatoes and continue to fry (uncovered) for another 5 minutes. Season generously with salt and pepper and set aside for 10 minutes or so to cool.

Break the eggs into a large bowl and beat lightly. Tip the contents of the frying pan and the Manchego into the beaten eggs and mix gently. Heat your 23–24-cm frying pan until moderately hot, add a little oil, wipe off the excess with kitchen towel, then pour in the egg mixture. Lift the edge of the tortilla as it begins to cook, letting the liquid egg run from the centre to the edge. Cook until most of the egg has set, then reduce the heat a little and cook for about 3–4 minutes. Meanwhile, preheat the grill to medium.

Slip the pan under the grill about 12 cm from the heat and leave until the top of the tortilla has puffed up and lightly browned and the egg in the middle has set (about 4 minutes). Remove from under the grill and leave to cool for about 30 minutes in the pan, then loosen it round the edge. Place a plate over the pan and flip the tortilla over so that it lands bottom-side upwards. Cut into wedges and serve at room temperature.

**What to drink:** This makes a good addition to a tapas selection so you could have a glass of manzanilla sherry with it.

# CHEESE AND BASIL SOUFFLES

Soufflés are one of the most impressive recipes you can make for your friends – guaranteed to provoke 'oohs' and 'aaahs' from everyone around the table, especially with this unusual combination of cheese and basil. They're not as difficult as they look – you just need to keep your nerve!

200 ml whole milk

4–6 sprigs of fresh basil
(depending how strong they are)

4 large eggs (or 5 if your whites are unusually small)

25 g butter

20 g plain flour

50 g mature Gruyère or Cheddar, grated

25 g mature Parmesan, freshly grated, plus extra to dust the soufflé dish

sea salt and freshly ground black pepper

*a 15-cm soufflé dish, 9 cm high,
lightly buttered*

**SERVES 4 AS A STARTER
OR 2 AS A MAIN COURSE**

Put the milk in a saucepan, add the basil sprigs and bring slowly to the boil. Turn the heat right down, simmer for 1 minute, then turn off the heat and leave the basil to infuse for about 20 minutes.

Separate the eggs carefully – put the whites in a large, clean bowl and set aside 3 of the yolks to add to the sauce.

Preheat the oven to 200°C (400°F) Gas 6.

Put a large, heavy-based saucepan over medium heat and add the butter. When that has melted, stir in the flour. Cook for a few seconds, then tip in the warm basil-infused milk through a sieve. Whisk together until smooth, then cook over low heat until thick.

Stir in the grated Gruyère and most of the Parmesan and put back over low heat until the cheese has melted. Leave to cool for 5 minutes. Stir in the 3 egg yolks one by one.

Sprinkle the inside of the buttered soufflé dish with a little Parmesan, shaking off any excess. Put the dish on a baking tray.

Whisk the egg whites and a pinch of salt until holding their shape but not stiff. Take 2 tablespoons of the whites and fold it into the cheese base, then carefully fold in the rest of the whites without overmixing. Tip the mixture into the prepared soufflé dish, scraping the last remnants in with a rubber spatula. Sprinkle with a little more Parmesan and bake in the preheated oven for 25–30 minutes until the soufflé is well risen and browned. (Don't open the oven door or your soufflé may collapse!) Serve immediately with some new potatoes or crusty bread and a green salad.

**Variation:** You can make these in individual ramekins, as shown opposite, if you prefer. In this case, bake them for 20–25 minutes.

**What to drink:** Champagne or other sparkling wines work extremely well with soufflés, or you could drink a smooth dry white, such as Chablis, Alsace Pinot Blanc or Gavi di Gavi.

# CHEDDAR AND CIDER FONDUE

Although the classic fondue recipe is Swiss, it's perfectly possible to make it with other cheeses. This one is one of my favourites, made from local West Country cheeses and Somerset cider. The key things to remember with fondue are to have your cheeses at room temperature before you start, to take the pan off the heat before adding the first batch of cheese and to stir in a figure-of-eight rather than round and round (which makes the fondue more likely to separate). Once you've got the knack, it's simplicity itself.

about 430 g thinly sliced or coarsely grated cheese, e.g. 150 g mature Cheddar, 150 g Double Gloucester and 130 g Somerset Brie (all rinds removed)

2 teaspoons cornflour or potato flour

175 ml dry but fruity cider, e.g. Sheppy's Dabinett

1 tablespoon medium-dry cider or Calvados

freshly ground white or black pepper

crusty wholemeal or granary rolls, cubed, to serve

apple wedges, to serve

*a cast-iron cheese fondue set*

**SERVES 2–3**

Toss the cheese with the cornflour. Set aside until it has come to room temperature.

Start off the fondue on your cooker. Pour the cider into your fondue pan and heat until almost boiling. Remove from the heat and tip in about one-third of the cheese. Keep breaking up the cheese with a wooden spoon using a figure-of-eight motion. (Stirring it round and round as you do with a sauce makes it more likely that the cheese will separate from the liquid).

Once the cheese has begun to melt, return it to a very low heat, stirring continuously. Gradually add the remaining cheese until you have a smooth, thick mass (this takes about 10 minutes, less with practice). If it seems too thick, add some more hot cider. Add the brandy and season with pepper (preferably white, as the grains won't show). Place over your fondue burner and serve with the cubes of bread. Use long fondue forks to dip the bread in, stirring the fondue often to prevent it solidifying. Have wedges of apple on hand to refresh you between mouthfuls of fondue.

**What to drink:** A dry or medium-dry cider will go perfectly.

# CHEESE AND SPICY BEAN BURRITOS WITH FRESH TOMATO SALSA

These are lighter than the baked burrito you tend to find in Mexican restaurants. They may look complicated to prepare but you can prepare the beans and salsa ahead of time and put them together at the last minute.

200 g mild, white crumbly cheese, e.g. Cheshire or Wensleydale

1 large avocado

freshly squeezed juice of 1 lemon or lime

1 tablespoon chopped fresh coriander leaves

4 large soft wheat tortillas or wraps

½ iceberg lettuce, finely shredded

sea salt and freshly ground black pepper

guacamole and soured cream, to serve (optional)

**SPICED BEANS**

2 tablespoons olive oil

½ bunch of spring onions, trimmed and thinly sliced

2 garlic cloves, crushed

1 teaspoon mild chilli powder

1 teaspoon ground cumin

1 large or 2 medium tinned tomatoes, plus 2 tablespoons of their juice, or 2 fresh tomatoes, skinned and roughly chopped

400-g tin kidney beans, drained and rinsed

2 heaped tablespoons chopped fresh coriander leaves

freshly squeezed lemon juice, to taste

**FRESH TOMATO SALSA**

350 g cherry tomatoes

2 spring onions, trimmed and thinly sliced

1 green chilli, deseeded and finely chopped

freshly squeezed juice of 1 lime

2 tablespoons chopped fresh coriander leaves

**SERVES 4**

First make the spiced beans. Put the oil in a saucepan over medium heat, then fry the spring onions for a couple of minutes. Stir in the garlic, chilli powder and cumin. Add the tomatoes, breaking them up with a spatula or wooden spoon. Tip in the beans, cover with a lid and cook for about 5–6 minutes until the liquid has evaporated. Take the pan off the heat and mash the beans roughly with a fork. Stir in the coriander and season with lemon juice and salt to taste. Set aside.

Next make the fresh tomato salsa. Chop up the cherry tomatoes and put them in a bowl with the spring onions, chilli and lime juice. Season with salt and stir in the coriander.

Now get the other ingredients ready. Crumble the cheese. Stone the avocado, then peel and chop the flesh into small cubes, toss with a little lime or lemon juice, season and stir in the coriander.

Warm a large frying pan over low heat and lay one of the tortillas in the pan. Leave to heat up for a minute, then turn it over and heat the other side. Lay it on a board and spread a quarter of the spiced beans in a large square in the middle. Top with a layer of crumbled cheese, then a layer of shredded lettuce. Spoon over a little of the salsa and scatter over a quarter of the avocado. Fold the sides of the tortilla to the middle, then carefully roll the burrito up from the edge nearest to you. Cut across diagonally with a sharp knife and arrange on a plate. Serve with generous dollops of guacamole and soured cream, if using, and more of the salsa.

**What to drink:** I actually enjoy a good lager with a burrito (see page 76) but a glass of Sauvignon Blanc or a dry rosé would also be enjoyable.

# IRRESISTIBLE ITALIAN FOUR-CHEESE PIZZA

**If, like me, you always reject the pizza 'quattro formaggi' as being bland and indigestible, just try making it with top-quality Italian cheeses.**

## PIZZA DOUGH

150 g strong white flour

125 g Italian '00' flour

1 teaspoon fine sea salt

1 teaspoon quick-acting yeast

½ teaspoon sugar

2 tablespoons olive oil, plus extra to drizzle

about 175 ml hand-hot water

semolina or cornmeal, to dust the baking trays

## PIZZA TOPPING

400 ml home-made* or good-quality, shop-bought Italian passata

150 g Pecorino Toscano (rind removed), sliced

150 g Taleggio (rind removed) or buffalo Mozzarella, sliced

90 g Gorgonzola piccante, crumbled

30 g mature Parmesan, freshly grated

a small handful of fresh oregano or basil leaves

freshly ground black pepper

*2 large baking trays, lightly oiled*

## MAKES 2 PIZZAS

To make the pizza dough, sift the 2 flours into a bowl along with the salt, yeast and sugar. Mix together, then form a hollow in the centre. Add the olive oil and half the hand-hot water and stir to incorporate the flour. Gradually add as much of the remaining water as you need to pull the dough together. (It should take most of it – you need a wettish dough.) Turn the dough out onto a board and knead for 10 minutes until smooth and elastic, adding a little extra flour to prevent the dough sticking if necessary. Put the dough into a lightly oiled bowl, cover with clingfilm and leave in a warm place until doubled in size, about 1–1¼ hours.

Preheat the oven to 240°C (475°F) Gas 9 and sprinkle the prepared baking trays with semolina.

Tip the dough out of the bowl and press down on it to knock out the air. Divide it in half. Pull and shape one piece of dough into a large circle, then place it on a prepared baking tray and push it out towards the edges of the tray. (It doesn't have to be a perfect circle!) Spread half the passata over the top, then arrange half the cheeses over the top. Season with pepper. Repeat with the other piece of dough and the remaining cheese. Drizzle a little olive oil over the top of each pizza and bake in the preheated oven for 8–10 minutes until the dough has puffed up and the cheese is brown and bubbling. Garnish the pizzas with oregano leaves and drizzle over a little more oil.

* To make home-made passata, heat 2 tablespoons olive oil in a large frying pan or wok, add 1 crushed garlic clove, fry for a few seconds, then add 1 level tablespoon tomato purée. Tip in 450 g chopped, skinned fresh ripe tomatoes and stir well. Cover with a lid and leave for 5 minutes to soften the tomatoes, then break them down with a fork or wooden spoon. Simmer, uncovered, for a further 5 minutes until the mixture is thick and pulpy. Season with salt, pepper and a pinch of sugar and leave to cool. (You can also make this with a 400-g tin of tomatoes, in which case you won't need the tomato purée.)

**What to drink:** A fruity Italian red, such as a young Chianti or Rosso di Montepulciano. (Red wine works much better with cooked than uncooked cheese.)

# TARTIFLETTE

**Tartiflette is a wickedly rich, sensationally good cheese and potato dish from the Savoie region of France. Perfect après-ski/cold weather fare.**

2 tablespoons sunflower or other light cooking oil

200 g smoked bacon lardons or diced smoked streaky bacon

2 large onions, thinly sliced (about 400 g)

2 large garlic cloves, thinly sliced

700 g waxy potatoes, e.g. Desirée, well scrubbed

a sprig of fresh rosemary (optional)

1 small or ½ large Reblochon (about 275 g)

150 ml double cream

freshly ground black pepper

*a large ovenproof dish, buttered*

**SERVES 6**

Heat the oil in a large frying pan and fry the lardons until beginning to brown. Remove from the pan with a slotted spoon. Tip in the onions, stir and fry over low heat for about 20–25 minutes until they have collapsed right down and are beginning to brown. Add the garlic about 5 minutes before the end of the cooking time. Meanwhile, cut the potatoes, unpeeled, into slices about ½ cm thick, place in a saucepan with the sprig of rosemary, if using, and cover with cold water. Bring to the boil and boil for 2 minutes, then remove the rosemary, drain the water and set the potatoes aside.

Preheat the oven to 200°C (400°F) Gas 6.

Cut the Reblochon into thin slices, removing the rind if you prefer. (If you have a very mature cheese with a sticky rind, you may prefer to remove it. I prefer to use a slightly younger cheese and keep the rind, which adds colour and texture.)

Tip half the potatoes into the baking dish, cover with half the onions and bacon and season with pepper. Repeat with the remaining potatoes, onions and bacon and pour over the cream. Distribute the Reblochon over the top of the dish, then bake in the preheated oven for 15–20 minutes until the cheese is brown and bubbling. Serve with a green salad.

**What to drink:** A crisp dry wine from Savoie or Switzerland would be ideal with this – the same sort of wine you would drink with a fondue.

# LEEK AND BLUE CHEESE QUICHE WITH HAZELNUT PASTRY

A good home-made quiche is a wonderful way to enjoy cheese. You can always use ready-made pastry to save time but this nutty pastry does have a great flavour. If you don't like blue cheese you could easily substitute Cheddar, Gouda or any other full-flavoured cheese. Do buy leeks that still have their green leaves rather than ready-trimmed ones.

3 leeks (about 400 g untrimmed)

40 g butter

3 large eggs

250 ml whipping cream

30 g mature Parmesan, freshly grated

100 g medium-strong blue cheese, e.g. Stilton, crumbled

sea salt and freshly ground black pepper

**HAZELNUT PASTRY**

25 g whole shelled hazelnuts

75 g plain flour

50 g wholemeal flour

75 g chilled butter, cubed

3–4 tablespoons iced water

*a deep 23-cm loose-based quiche tin*
*baking beans*

**SERVES 4–6**

Preheat the oven to 190°C (375°F) Gas 5.

First make the pastry. Put the hazelnuts on a baking tray and roast in the preheated oven for 10 minutes or until the skins turn dark brown. (Turn off the oven.) Leave to cool for a few minutes, then tip them onto a clean tea towel and rub off the skins. Transfer to a food processor and pulse until finely chopped but not powdery, then add the flours and pulse once or twice to mix. Add the butter and pulse to incorporate, then add just enough of the iced water to bring the mixture together. Pat the pastry into a ball, wrap in clingfilm and leave to rest in the fridge for 1 hour.

Meanwhile, trim the bases and cut the coarse outer leaves from the leeks. Thinly slice the leeks and rinse thoroughly to get rid of any dirt or grit. Heat the butter in a large frying pan and fry the leeks for 5–6 minutes until beginning to soften. Season well and set aside to cool.

Roll the pastry out to a circle big enough to fit your quiche tin. Carefully lower the pastry into the tin, pressing it into the edges, and lightly prick the base with a fork. Leave any overhanging pastry untrimmed. Refrigerate for 20 minutes. Preheat the oven again to 190°C (375°F) Gas 5.

Line the pastry case with greaseproof paper, fill with baking beans and bake in the preheated oven for about 12 minutes. Leave the oven on.

Separate 1 of the eggs, reserve the white and beat the yolk and the other 2 whole eggs together. Measure the cream in a jug, add the beaten egg and half the Parmesan, season with pepper and beat well.

Remove the paper and beans from the pastry case and brush lightly with the reserved egg white. Return to the oven for another 5 minutes, then remove from the oven and reduce the oven temperature to 180°C (350°F) Gas 4. Trim the overhanging edge of pastry with a sharp knife. Scatter half the blue cheese in the pastry case, spoon over the leeks, then cover with the remaining blue cheese. Carefully pour the egg and cream mixture evenly over the top (only use as much as you need to fill the case). Sprinkle over the remaining Parmesan. Bake for about 35–40 minutes until the top is puffed up and lightly browned. Leave to cool for about 20 minutes before serving. (I personally think it's nicest at room temperature.)

**What to drink:** Cider is always good with leeks, or a smooth dry white wine like a subtly oaked Chardonnay, a Pinot Blanc or a Chenin Blanc.

# SAFFRON RISOTTO WITH AGED PARMESAN, SAGE AND SERRANO HAM

**A good risotto depends on good ingredients, so make sure you have a well-flavoured stock, good-quality ham and well-aged Parmesan (or Grana Padano) cheese.**

600 ml chicken stock, preferably home-made

40 g butter

1 small onion or ½ medium onion, finely chopped

175 g arborio or other Italian risotto rice

½ glass (about 75 ml) dry white wine

a Parmesan rind (optional)

a small pinch (about ¼ teaspoon) saffron strands

1–2 tablespoons jellied meat juices* (optional)

25 g aged Parmesan, freshly grated, plus a few Parmesan shavings

2 tablespoons olive oil

2–3 slices of Serrano or other Spanish air-dried ham, each torn into 3

8–10 fresh sage leaves

sea salt and freshly ground black pepper

**SERVES 2**

Bring the stock to the boil, then leave it simmering on a low heat.

Melt 25 g of the butter over medium heat in a large saucepan, add the onion and cook gently until soft, about 5 minutes. Tip in the rice, stir and cook for 2–3 minutes until the grains have turned opaque and are beginning to catch on the bottom of the pan. Add the wine, stir and let it bubble up and evaporate.

Add the Parmesan rind if you have one, then begin to add the hot stock, adding about a coffee cup at a time and allowing the liquid to be absorbed by the rice before you add the next lot. Cook, stirring regularly, until the rice begins to look creamy but still has some bite to it, about 20 minutes. Pour the last bit of stock over the saffron and add to the risotto along with a couple of spoonfuls of jellied meat juices, if you have some. Turn off the heat, add the remaining butter and the grated Parmesan and stir. Cover the pan and let the flavours amalgamate for 2–3 minutes.

Heat the oil in a frying pan and quickly fry the ham. Remove from the pan with a slotted spoon and drain on a piece of kitchen paper. Fry the sage leaves in the same pan until crisp. Give the risotto a final stir, remove the Parmesan rind and season to taste. Serve in warm, shallow soup bowls and top with the crisp ham, sage leaves and a few shavings of Parmesan.

* What you want are the umami-rich meat juices which collect under the fat you pour off when you're cooking a chicken or a pork or veal joint.

**What to drink:** A glass of dry Italian white wine, such as a Soave.

# EXTRA-CRISPY MACARONI CHEESE

The best bit about macaroni cheese, as we all know, is the crispy topping, and it suddenly struck me how wonderful it would be to have crispy bits all the way through. It is, and this is how you do it.

125–150 g strong Cheddar, coarsely grated
25 g butter
25 g plain flour
300 ml whole milk
175 g rigatoni or penne
½ teaspoon English mustard or 1 teaspoon Dijon mustard
a few drops of Worcestershire sauce
sea salt and freshly ground black pepper

*a shallow ovenproof dish, lightly buttered*

**SERVES 2–3**

Preheat the oven to 170°C (325°F) Gas 3.

Sprinkle 50 g of the Cheddar in an even layer over a baking tray. Bake in the preheated oven for 8–10 minutes until bubbling and beginning to brown. Remove from the oven, leave to cool, then break into pieces.

Put the butter in a medium non-stick saucepan and melt gently. Stir in the flour and cook for a few seconds, then take the pan off the heat and add the milk little by little, stirring before you add the next amount. Put the pan back on the hob, increase the heat slightly, then bring the sauce gradually to the boil, stirring continuously. Turn the heat right down again and leave the sauce to simmer for 5 minutes, stirring it occasionally.

Bring a large saucepan of water to the boil, add salt, then tip in the pasta. Cook according to the manufacturer's instructions. Meanwhile, preheat the grill.

Just before the pasta is ready, stir half the remaining Cheddar into the sauce, add the mustard and Worcestershire sauce and season to taste. Add a little more milk if it looks too thick.

Drain the pasta thoroughly and tip into the prepared ovenproof dish. Scatter the crispy cheese pieces over the pasta and mix together. Pour in the cheese sauce, then sprinkle over the remaining Cheddar. Place the dish under the hot grill for about 5 minutes until the top is brown and crispy.

**What to drink:** A medium-bodied fruity red, such as a Saint-Emilion or other fruity Merlot, works very well.

# MAC 'N' GREENS

A healthy spin on macaroni cheese which can be used as a side for a roast or grilled meat.

50 g butter
1 medium/large leek, trimmed and thinly sliced
40 g plain flour
600 ml semi-skimmed milk
a head of broccoli divided into small florets (about 300 g florets)
350 g penne (plain or wholewheat)
2 handfuls of chard or spinach leaves
150 g mature Gruyère
3 heaped tablespoons freshly grated Parmesan
sea salt, freshly ground black pepper and grated nutmeg

*4 or 6 individual ovenproof dishes, lightly buttered*

**SERVES 4 AS A MAIN COURSE OR 6 AS A SIDE**

Put the butter in a medium non-stick saucepan and melt gently. Add the leeks, stir and cook for 1 minute, then stir in the flour and cook for a few seconds. Take the pan off the heat and gradually add the milk, stirring continuously. Put the pan back on the hob, increase the heat slightly, then bring the milk gradually up to simmering point. Turn the heat right down again and leave the sauce over very low heat.

Fill a large saucepan with boiling water from the kettle, bring back to the boil, add salt, then add the broccoli and blanch for a couple of minutes. Transfer the broccoli to a sieve with a slotted spoon and rinse with cold water. Tip the pasta into the same water in the pan and cook for the time recommended on the pack.

Wash and remove the stalk and central rib from the chard or spinach (unless using baby leaves). Just before the pasta is ready, stir half the Gruyère and the Parmesan into the sauce and check the seasoning, adding salt, pepper, nutmeg and more Parmesan, if necessary. Add the broccoli and chard or spinach, stir and set aside for 3–4 minutes. Preheat the grill.

Drain the pasta and divide between the prepared ovenproof dishes. Pour over the sauce and vegetables and mix gently, then sprinkle over the remaining Gruyère. Place the dishes on a baking tray and grill for 5 minutes until the cheese is brown and bubbling.

**What to drink:** If you're making this as a side for grilled pork or veal, serve a medium-bodied Italian red. An unoaked Chardonnay or Italian white like a Soave would work well with it on its own.

PAGE 119 *Extra-crispy Macaroni Cheese*
RIGHT *Mac 'n' Greens*

# CHARD, ONION AND PARMESAN GRATIN

You may be tempted to discard the fleshy white central rib of chard leaves but they make a delicate-tasting gratin that can be served as a side vegetable or, with the addition of ham, as a main course dish.

1 tablespoon olive oil

25 g butter

1 medium/large onion, roughly chopped

1 teaspoon finely chopped fresh thyme leaves or ½ teaspoon dried thyme

stalks from a large bunch of chard, washed, trimmed and sliced, plus 4 chard leaves, roughly shredded

1 tablespoon plain flour

150 ml whole milk

1 tablespoon crème fraîche or double cream (optional)

30 g Grana Padano or Parmesan, freshly grated, plus 3 tablespoons for the topping

2 tablespoons fresh breadcrumbs (optional)

sea salt and freshly ground black pepper

*a medium ovenproof dish*

**SERVES 2 AS A MAIN COURSE OR 4 AS A SIDE**

Heat a non-stick saucepan, add the oil and 15 g of the butter and tip in the onion. Cover with a lid and cook over low heat for about 5–6 minutes until beginning to soften. Stir in the thyme, then add the chard stalks and cook for another 3–4 minutes. Season. Preheat the grill.

Stir in the flour, then add the milk, bring to the boil and simmer until the sauce has thickened. Stir in the chard leaves and cook for 1 minute, then add the crème fraîche and cheese. Tip into the ovenproof dish. Mix the remaining 3 tablespoons cheese with the breadcrumbs, if using, and scatter over the gratin. Chop the remaining butter into little pieces and dot over the top. Grill until brown and bubbling.

**Variation:** You could also add some chopped ham if you wanted to turn this into a main course dish.

**What to drink:** If serving this as a vegetable side, be guided by the main course, otherwise a smooth dry white wine, such as a Chardonnay, will work well.

LEFT *Chard, Onion and Parmesan Gratin*

# MUSHROOM DAUPHINOIS

Adding mushrooms and extra cheese to this gorgeously creamy French potato classic makes it substantial enough to serve on its own, as well as being the perfect accompaniment for roast lamb.

40 g butter, cubed, plus a little extra for the topping

250 g chestnut mushrooms, wiped, trimmed and sliced

1 teaspoon finely chopped fresh thyme leaves (optional)

300 ml whipping cream, or 225 ml double cream and 75 ml whole milk

2 garlic cloves, thinly sliced

600 g waxy potatoes, e.g. Desirée

50 g Gruyère, Beaufort or Comté, finely grated

15 g Parmesan, freshly grated

sea salt and freshly ground black pepper

*a shallow ovenproof dish, buttered*

**SERVES 6**

Preheat the oven to 190°C (375°F) Gas 5.

Heat a large frying pan or wok and add the butter. When it has melted and stopped foaming, tip in the mushrooms. Fry for a couple of minutes, then stir-fry until lightly browned. Stir in the thyme and remove from the heat.

Pour the cream into a small saucepan and heat very gently with the garlic. Turn off the heat and leave to infuse while you peel the potatoes and cut them into very thin slices.

Arrange a layer of potatoes over the bottom of the prepared ovenproof dish. Tip half the mushrooms over the potatoes, sprinkle over half the Gruyère and season with salt and pepper. Put another layer of potatoes on top, then the remaining mushrooms and Gruyère and season again. Top with the remaining potatoes. Carefully pour over the infused cream, distributing it evenly over the dish. Sprinkle the top with Parmesan. Chop a small slice of butter into little pieces and dot over the top. Bake in the preheated oven for 1 hour–1 hour 15 minutes until the top is browned and the potatoes thoroughly cooked. Leave to rest for at least 5 minutes before serving.

**What to drink:** Most medium-bodied reds would work well with this – Pinot Noir would be particularly delicious.

# WARM PEAR, GORGONZOLA AND PECAN TARTLETS WITH MAPLE DRIZZLE

A cheese course and dessert rolled into one – a fabulous finale for a dinner party.

375 g ready-rolled puff pastry
1 egg, lightly beaten
200 g Gorgonzola
4 tablespoons double cream
2–3 ripe pears
75 g shelled pecan nuts or walnuts
6 teaspoons maple syrup
cayenne pepper

**SERVES 6**

Preheat the oven to 220°C (425°F) Gas 7.

Take the pastry out of the fridge and leave to warm up a little for 10–15 minutes.

Unroll the pastry, cut it in half horizontally, then cut each of the halves into 3 to make 6 equal-sized pieces. With the tip of a sharp knife, score round each of the squares about 1.5 cm from the edge to make a border. Lightly brush the border with beaten egg, taking care not to brush over the cut you've made (otherwise the pastry won't puff up around the edge of the tartlets).

Put the Gorgonzola in a bowl and break up roughly with a fork, then stir in the cream. Season with a little cayenne pepper and spread over the bases of the tartlets, taking care not to cover the border. Roughly break up the pecan nuts and divide between the tartlets. Peel, core and quarter the pears, cut each quarter into 3 wedges and lay them in slices on top of the cheese and nuts. Drizzle a teaspoonful of maple syrup over each tart and bake in the preheated oven for 15–20 minutes until the pastry is well browned and puffed up. Leave to cool for 5 minutes before serving.

**What to drink:** A glass of lightly chilled young tawny port or an Australian Liqueur Muscat would be delicious with these.

*LEFT Warm Pear, Gorgonzola and Pecan Tartlets with Maple Drizzle*

# LAVENDER HONEY AND VANILLA CHEESECAKE

An extremely easy and delicious cheesecake. If you can't find lavender honey, use any fragrant honey like Acacia or Orange Blossom – or a regular clear honey.

350 g fromage frais (not the reduced-fat version)
350 g curd cheese
2 teaspoons vanilla extract
25 g golden caster sugar
3 large eggs, beaten
3 tablespoons lavender honey, acacia honey or other aromatic clear honey, or to taste

**BASE**
150 g sweet oat biscuits
55 g butter
1 teaspoon ground cinnamon

*a 20-cm loose-based springform cake tin*

**SERVES 8**

Preheat the oven to 150°C (300°F) Gas 2. Pour any liquid off the fromage frais and tip into a sieve to drain while you make the base.

To make the base, put the biscuits in a plastic bag and crush with a rolling pin until you have even-sized crumbs. Melt the butter in a small saucepan, stir in the cinnamon, cook for a few seconds, then stir in the biscuit crumbs until they have absorbed all the butter. Tip into the cake tin and distribute evenly. Press down well with the back of a spoon. Place the tin on a baking tray and bake in the preheated oven for 20 minutes until crisp.

Tip the curd cheese and drained fromage frais into a large bowl. Add the vanilla extract, sugar and one-third of the eggs and whisk until smooth. Whisk in the remaining eggs. Dip a tablespoon into a mug of boiling water, then add the honey to the cheesecake, a spoonful at a time and dipping the spoon back into the hot water in between each spoonful. Whisk the honey into the cheesecake topping and check for sweetness, adding another spoonful if needed. Pour the mixture onto the base, put back in the oven and bake for 30 minutes until just firm. Turn off the oven and leave the cheesecake to cool, then cover with clingfilm and refrigerate for at least 2 hours or overnight. Serve with plum, apricot or rhubarb compote and a dusting of icing sugar.

**What to drink:** Cheesecake needs a sweet wine with pronounced acidity to offset its richness. A Beerenauslese Chardonnay or a late-harvest Sauvignon Blanc would both work well.

THIS PAGE *Lavender Honey and Vanilla Cheesecake*
RIGHT *Lemon and Blueberry Upside-down Cheesecakes*

# LEMON AND BLUEBERRY UPSIDE-DOWN CHEESECAKES

A gorgeous sweet, lemony version of the fashionable French verrine (see page 88) and really easy to make.

110 g digestive biscuits
55 g butter
1 teaspoon ground cinnamon
250 g mascarpone
3–4 tablespoons home-made or good-quality shop-bought lemon curd
2–3 tablespoons semi-skimmed milk
2–3 teaspoons freshly squeezed lemon juice, strained
250 g fresh or frozen blueberries

*a baking tin*
*4–6 small tumblers*

**SERVES 4–6**

Preheat the oven to 190°C (375°F) Gas 5.

Put the biscuits in a plastic bag and crush with a rolling pin until you have even-sized crumbs. (You can do this in a food processor but it tends to make them a bit fine and powdery.) Melt the butter in a small saucepan, stir in the cinnamon, cook for a few seconds, then stir in the biscuit crumbs until they have absorbed all the butter. Tip into the baking tin and bake in the preheated oven for 5 minutes until the crumbs are crisp. Set aside to cool.

Tip the mascarpone into a bowl and mix in the lemon curd with a wooden spoon until smooth. (Don't use an electric beater – it will make the mixture seize up and become too buttery.) Add the milk to give a softer, more spoonable consistency and a little lemon juice to adjust the sweetness.

Divide the blueberries between the tumblers. Spoon over the mascarpone mixture and top with the biscuit crumbs. Cover the glasses with clingfilm and refrigerate for an hour or so. (The bases can be made further in advance but don't add the crumble topping too far ahead otherwise it will go soggy.)

* You can vary this idea with other curds and fruits. A raspberry curd and mascarpone mixture, for example, would be delicious with fresh raspberries underneath; a lime curd with chopped kiwi fruit; or an orange curd with mandarin oranges.

**What to drink:** A late-harvest, Beerenauslese or vendange tardive Riesling would go well with this.

# RASPBERRY AND RICOTTA HOTCAKES

This is my spin on what has become a modern classic. They are feather-light, fruity pancakes, perfect for a romantic breakfast or brunch.

200 g fresh or part-thawed raspberries
3 tablespoons caster sugar
110 g ricotta
2 eggs, separated
75 ml whole milk
60 g plain flour
½ teaspoon baking powder
a pinch of salt
25 g butter
crème fraîche or double cream, to serve (optional)

**SERVES 2–4** (DEPENDING HOW HUNGRY OR GREEDY YOU ARE)

Set aside 75 g of the raspberries and put the remainder in a small saucepan with 2 tablespoons of the sugar. Set over low heat and leave until the sugar has melted and the raspberries start to bubble up. (Add a little more water if necessary.) Set aside.

Put the ricotta in a bowl with the remaining sugar and the egg yolks, beat together with a wooden spoon, then mix in the milk. Sift the flour, baking powder and salt into the ricotta mixture and stir in.

Gently melt the butter in a small saucepan over low heat.

Whisk the egg whites in a clean bowl with an electric handheld whisk until stiff. Fold a heaped tablespoon of the egg whites into the ricotta mixture to loosen it. Lightly fold in the remaining egg whites and the raspberries you've set aside.

Heat a frying pan, pour in a little of the melted butter, then drop 2–3 tablespoons of the batter into the pan. Let the hotcake cook for a couple of minutes over low heat, then carefully turn it over with a palette knife and cook the other side. Cook the remaining hotcakes in the same way, adding a little more butter to the pan each time. Hand the hotcakes out straightaway with the warm raspberry sauce and a bowl of crème fraîche or jug of double cream (not that it really needs it but it's extra-delicious this way!)

**What to drink:** Delicious with a cappuccino for breakfast or with a glass of Prosecco for a brunch.

*RIGHT Raspberry and Ricotta Hotcakes*

# PARMESAN AND CRISP BACON SCONES

**These light, airy little scones are so easy to rustle up and make a delicious snack.**

1 tablespoon sunflower oil

2 rashers of streaky bacon, rinded and finely chopped

225 g self-raising flour

2 teaspoons baking powder

¼ teaspoon salt

a pinch of cayenne pepper

25 g mature Parmesan, freshly grated

40 g chilled butter, cubed

1 egg, plus enough semi-skimmed milk to make 150 ml liquid

extra milk, to glaze (optional)

cream cheese or mascarpone, to serve

*a 5-cm scone/biscuit cutter*

*a large baking tray, lightly oiled and dusted with flour*

**SERVES 4**

Preheat the oven to 220°C (425°F) Gas 7.

Heat the oil in a frying pan and fry the bacon over moderate heat until crisp. Set aside to cool.

Sift the flour, baking powder, salt and cayenne pepper into a large bowl. Rub in the butter with your fingertips, keeping the mixture as light as possible. Stir in the Parmesan and bacon.

Make a well in the centre and pour in most of the egg and milk mixture, pulling the mixture together as you go. Add just enough egg mixture to bring everything together into a dough, then stop. (You can do all this in a food processor, if you like.) Turn the dough out onto a lightly floured work surface and lightly press it into a rough circle about 2.5 cm thick. Stamp out the scones with your cutter, pressing the offcuts of dough lightly together to make the last few scones. Brush the scones lightly with milk or the remaining egg and milk mixture and put on the prepared baking tray. Bake in the preheated oven for 15 minutes until well risen and lightly browned. Turn out onto a wire rack to cool completely. To serve, split and spread with cream cheese or mascarpone.

LEFT *Parmesan and Crisp Bacon Scones*

# DOUBLE CHEESE AND BACON MUFFINS

**These irresistibly gooey, cheesy muffins are very simple to make – you just need to take care not to overmix them.**

2 tablespoons sunflower oil

100 g streaky bacon, very finely chopped

1 onion, finely chopped

100 g butter, cubed

300 g plain flour

1 tablespoon baking powder

½ teaspoon salt

2 heaped tablespoons natural unsweetened yoghurt

about 125 ml whole milk

3 eggs, lightly beaten

25 g mature Parmesan, freshly grated, plus a little extra for the topping

125 g mature Cheddar, diced

*a non-stick muffin tin with 12 deep holes or a regular muffin tin lined with non-stick paper cases*

**MAKES 12 LARGE MUFFINS**

Heat the oil in a frying pan and fry the bacon until the fat begins to run. Add the onion and continue to cook over low heat until the onion is lightly browned. Set aside and leave to cool.

Gently melt the butter in a small saucepan over low heat.

Preheat the oven to 190°C (375°F) Gas 5.

Sif the flour, baking powder and salt into a large bowl, then sift it again and make a well in the centre. Put the yoghurt in a measuring jug and mix in enough milk to make up 225 ml.

Pour the melted butter, eggs and yoghurt and milk mixture into the flour along with the Parmesan. Mix in lightly and swiftly with a large metal spoon to create a rough batter. (This should only take a few seconds – do not overmix otherwise the finished muffins will be tough.) Fold in the bacon, onion and Cheddar. Spoon the batter into the holes or paper cases in the muffin tin and sprinkle with a little more Parmesan. Bake in the preheated oven for about 25–30 minutes or until fully risen and well browned. Leave in the tin for 5 minutes, then transfer to a wire rack for another 10–15 minutes to cool slightly. Eat warm with soup or a salad.

# TOASTED SEED AND FENNEL BREAD

Toasted seeds, especially fennel seeds, are particularly good with cheese, so try incorporating them into this easy, tasty bread.

2 tablespoons fennel seeds
250 g strong white flour, plus a little extra to dust
150 g strong wholemeal flour
100 g rye flour
1½ teaspoons easy-blend or quick-acting yeast
1½ teaspoons fine sea salt
50 g mixed toasted seeds, plus extra to sprinkle
1 tablespoon malt extract
310 ml hand-hot water
2 tablespoons sunflower or rapeseed oil

*a baking tray, lightly oiled*

**MAKES 1 MEDIUM LOAF**

Warm the fennel seeds over low heat in a dry frying pan until they begin to change colour and yield their fragrance. Set aside and leave to cool.

Mix together the flours in a large bowl. Stir in the yeast, salt and mixed toasted seeds, including the fennel seeds. Dissolve the malt extract in 2 tablespoons of the hand-hot water. Make a well in the centre of the flour and pour in the malt extract and water, the sunflower oil and the rest of the water. Start working the flour into the liquid with a wooden spoon, then mix with your hands until all the flour is incorporated.

Turn the dough out onto a lightly floured work surface and knead for 7–8 minutes until the dough begins to feel elastic. Place the dough in a large bowl covered with a clean, dampened tea towel and leave for about 45–50 minutes until doubled in size.

Tip the dough out of the bowl and press down on it to knock out the air. Roll up the dough into a long oval, tucking in the ends to neaten the shape. Place on the prepared baking tray, make 4 diagonal cuts in the top with a sharp knife, cover with the tea towel and leave for another 25 minutes. Meanwhile, preheat the oven to 200°C (400°F) Gas 6.

Brush the top of the loaf lightly with water and sprinkle a couple of tablespoons of mixed toasted seeds over it. Bake in the preheated oven for about 35–40 minutes until the loaf is well browned and sounds hollow when you tap it on the base. Leave to cool on a wire rack for a good 45 minutes before serving.

# QUICK COURGETTE, FETA AND MINT BREAD

Quick, flavoured breads like this are hugely popular in France where they refer to them as 'cake'. In fact, they're more like a cross between a quiche and a bread, nice to serve with a bowl of soup or cut into cubes as a pre-dinner nibble with a glass of wine.

25 g butter
4 spring onions, trimmed and thinly sliced
300 g courgettes, trimmed and coarsely grated
2 tablespoons finely chopped fresh mint leaves
175 g plain flour
1 tablespoon baking powder
3 large eggs, beaten
100 ml long-life milk
100 ml light olive oil
150 g Feta, crumbled into small pieces
sea salt and freshly ground black pepper

*a 23 x 11-cm non-stick loaf tin, lightly oiled and dusted with flour*

**SERVES 6**

Preheat the oven to 180°C (350°F) Gas 4.

Heat a large frying pan or wok and add the butter. When it has melted and stopped foaming, tip in the spring onions and courgettes. Stir-fry over high heat for 1 minute, then remove from the heat and stir in the mint. Leave to cool for about 20 minutes, then strain off any excess liquid.

Sift the flour and baking powder into a bowl and season well. Whisk the eggs, milk and oil in another bowl, then tip two-thirds of it into the flour. Beat well, then add the remaining egg mixture. Mix in the Feta and fried spring onions and courgettes, then transfer to the prepared loaf tin. Bake in the preheated oven for 50 minutes or until a skewer inserted in the middle comes out clean. Leave to cool, then remove from the tin. If not serving immediately, wrap in foil and store in the fridge. Serve at room temperature, sliced and cut into halves or squares.

**What to drink:** A glass of crisp Sauvignon Blanc, such as a Sancerre, would go particularly well with this.

**RIGHT** *Toasted Seed and Fennel Bread*

# TALEGGIO AND GRAPE FOCACCIA

**This gorgeously gooey bread makes a great accompaniment for a selection of antipasti.**

250 g strong white flour

250 g Italian '00' flour

1 teaspoon quick-acting yeast

1 teaspoon golden caster sugar

2 teaspoons fine sea salt

300 ml hand-hot water

2–3 tablespoons olive oil,
plus extra to drizzle

30 g Parmesan, freshly grated

175 g Taleggio (rind removed), thinly sliced

75 g Gorgonzola, thinly sliced

150 g red seedless grapes

2 sprigs of fresh rosemary, torn into pieces

a little fine or coarse semolina (optional)

coarse sea salt and freshly ground
black pepper

*an 18 x 32-cm baking tin, lightly greased and
dusted with fine semolina, if using*

**SERVES 6–8**

Put the flours, yeast, sugar and salt in a large bowl. Mix well, then make a well in the centre. Pour in the hand-hot water and 1 tablespoon of the olive oil, then bring the mixture together, first with a wooden spoon and then with your hands. Add a little extra water, if necessary. Tip the dough out onto a lightly floured work surface and knead until smooth and it springs back when you press it with a finger, about 5–6 minutes. Put in a lightly oiled bowl, cover with clingfilm and leave to rise for about 45 minutes or until doubled in size.

Tip the dough out of the bowl and press down on it to knock out the air. Give it a couple of swift turns on the work surface, then divide in half but make one half slightly bigger than the other. Stretch and press the larger of the 2 halves into the prepared baking tin so that it covers the base and comes up the sides. Sprinkle over the Parmesan, then add the sliced Taleggio and Gorgonzola and cover with the grapes. Season well with pepper. Roll out and stretch the other piece of dough to fit over the filling, bringing up the dough underneath and pressing to seal round the sides. Cover with clingfilm or a tea towel and leave for another 30 minutes or so to rise.

Fifteen minutes before you think the dough will be ready, preheat the oven to 220°C (425°F) Gas 7.

Using the tips of your fingers, make deep indentations in the dough, taking care not to deflate the whole bread, and push the rosemary into the holes. Brush the surface with the remaining olive oil and season with coarse salt. Bake in the preheated oven for 10 minutes, then reduce the heat to 200°C (400°F) Gas 6 and cook for another 15 minutes until the bread is well risen and golden. Drizzle with a little more olive oil, leave to cool for 5–10 minutes, then cut into squares or strips.

# CHEDDAR AND CRACKED PEPPER STRAWS

Cheese straws are a great way to use up the last bits and pieces of hard cheese, particularly a good tangy Cheddar.

150 g plain flour
¼ teaspoon English mustard powder
a pinch of sea salt
100 g chilled unsalted butter, cubed
150 g strong, mature farmhouse Cheddar, coarsely grated
2 tablespoons coarsely ground black pepper
1 egg yolk

*1–2 baking trays, lightly oiled*

**SERVES 6–8**

Sift the flour, mustard powder and salt into a bowl. Cut in the butter and rub together with your fingertips as if you were making pastry. Add the Cheddar and pepper and rub in thoroughly. Beat the egg yolk with 2 tablespoons water and add just enough of this mixture to the flour to enable you to pull it together into a dough. Shape into a flat disc, wrap in clingfilm and refrigerate for 30 minutes, then take out and leave to come back to room temperature.

Preheat the oven to 190°C (375°F) Gas 5.

Roll out the dough thinly, then cut into strips about 30 cm long. (Don't cut off the uneven ends – that's what makes them look home-made!) Lay the strips carefully on the prepared baking trays and bake in the preheated oven for 12–15 minutes until golden brown. Leave on the trays for 10 minutes, then carefully transfer to a wire rack to finish cooling. Eat fresh, ideally, but they will keep well for a couple of days in an airtight container (you can refresh them briefly in a warm oven).

# OAT BISCUITS FOR CHEESE

I came across these in a London restaurant, The Greenhouse, which prides itself on its cheese board. Chef Antonin Bonnet created them to complement a wide range of cheeses, a task it very successfully fulfils.

210 g plain flour
50 g buckwheat flour
½ teaspoon bicarbonate of soda
1½ teaspoons fine sea salt
¼ teaspoon finely ground white or black pepper
250 g softened butter, cubed
3 egg whites (100 ml)
160 g rolled oats

*biscuit cutters in different sizes*
*several baking trays lined with non-stick baking parchment*

**MAKES ABOUT 45 BISCUITS**

Sift the flours, bicarbonate of soda, salt and pepper into a bowl. Put the butter and egg whites in a food processor and whizz until smooth. Add half the flour mixture and pulse to amalgamate, then the remaining flour and finally the oats. (If your processor isn't big enough, tip the mixture into a large bowl once you've added the first lot of flour and add the rest of the flour and the oats by hand). Form the dough into a flat disc, wrap in clingfilm and leave to rest in the fridge for at least 1 hour.

Preheat the oven to 190°C (375°F) Gas 5.

Divide the dough into 4. Roll each quarter out thinly and stamp out rounds with the cutters (I like to make these in different sizes). Transfer carefully to the prepared baking trays and bake in the preheated oven for 12–15 minutes until lightly coloured and crisp.

# LABNEH WITH HERBS, RAW VEGETABLES AND FLATBREAD

Cheese is surprisingly easy to make. This is a Middle Eastern version that simply requires some yoghurt, salt and a muslin cloth. Depending on how long you let the cheese drain, you can create a soft, spreadable, dunkable cheese or a slightly firmer one that you can roll into balls. Either makes a stylish and unusual light meal.

2 large 450–500-g pots natural, full-fat unsweetened yoghurt

1 scant teaspoon fine sea salt

### TO SERVE

extra virgin olive oil

2 heaped tablespoons chopped fresh flat leaf parsley, coriander and mint leaves

strips of raw carrot, cucumber and celery

black and green olives

Sardinian crisp flatbread and warm pitta bread strips

*a large square of muslin*

*kitchen string*

### SERVES 4–6

Lay the square of muslin over a large bowl. Mix together the yoghurt and salt, then tip carefully into the lined bowl. Pull the edges of the muslin square together and tie securely with kitchen string to form a bundle. Hang over the bowl or the sink and leave for about 12–16 hours.

If using straightaway, tip the drained cheese from the muslin into a bowl and make a shallow dip in the centre. Drizzle over some olive oil, scatter with the chopped herbs and serve with the raw vegetables, olives and flatbread. If eating it later, you can store it in the fridge in a covered bowl or box for up to 36 hours.

* If you don't want to make this labneh from scratch, you can get a similar result by mixing 2 parts natural yoghurt to 1 part cream cheese.

# LABNEH BALLS WITH DUKKAH

You can roll these easy labneh balls in home-made dukkah or the same freshly chopped herbs used to serve the Labneh (left). You could also preserve them, uncoated, in a jar of olive oil in the same way as the Feta recipe opposite.

1 recipe Labneh (see left)

### DUKKAH

125 g whole, skinned almonds or a mixture of almonds and hazelnuts

25 g coriander seeds

10–12 g cumin seeds

75 g sesame seeds

1 teaspoon sea salt

½ teaspoon black peppercorns

1 teaspoon dried oregano

### MAKES ABOUT 250 G

Prepare the labneh following the recipe on the left, but leave to drain for an extra 12 hours or so until firm. Roll the thoroughly drained cheese into walnut-sized balls.

To make the dukkah, preheat the oven to 180°C (350°F) Gas 4.

Lay the almonds (and hazelnuts, if using) and coriander, cumin and sesame seeds separately on baking trays or in baking tins. Roast in the preheated oven until lightly coloured and fragrant – about 7–8 minutes for the nuts, 5 minutes for the coriander seeds, 4 minutes for the cumin seeds and 3–4 minutes for the sesame seeds. Set aside and leave to cool.

With a pestle and mortar, grind together the sea salt with the peppercorns and oregano. If you feel energetic, you can grind the coriander and cumin seeds too (you'll need to do this in batches).

Chop the almonds (and hazelnuts) roughly, then tip them into a food processor. Pulse to break them up, then add the sesame seeds and coriander and cumin seeds, if you haven't already ground them. Process again until you have a roughly textured mixture that looks like coarse breadcrumbs. Add the oregano mix and pulse once to amalgamate. Store in an airtight tin.

Roll the labneh balls in the dukkah or alternatively in mixed, chopped fresh herbs as suggested above.

PAGE 139 *Labneh with olive oil, olives and flat leaf parsley*

# MARINATED FETA WITH HERBS

You can buy Feta ready-marinated but if you do it yourself it will look and taste much better.

2 bay leaves

a few sprigs of fresh wild thyme and rosemary

1 fine strip of lemon or orange zest

200 g Feta, cut into large cubes

1 teaspoon mixed or black peppercorns, lightly crushed

1–2 dried chillies (optional)

500 ml extra virgin olive oil

*1–2 wide-necked preserving jars, sterilized (see page 4)*

**SERVES 3–4**

Put the bay leaves, thyme, rosemary and lemon zest in a small saucepan of boiling water and blanch for 30 seconds. Remove with a slotted spoon and set aside to cool.

Layer the Feta cubes in the preserving jar(s), tucking the herbs, zest, peppercorns and chillies between them. Pour over enough olive oil to cover the cheese completely. Put a lid on the jar(s) and store in the fridge for 2–3 days. Bring to room temperature before serving and use within 2 weeks.

* For a quicker result, you can marinate Feta in olive oil and a little lemon juice and flavour it with chopped fresh mint or dried oregano and finely chopped chilli, but it won't keep.

# PEARS IN PINOT NOIR

**Poached pears (or plums) in red wine make a delicious accompaniment for a creamy blue cheese.**

3 Conference pears

75–100 g soft light brown sugar (depending how ripe and fruity the wine is)

375 ml inexpensive Pinot Noir

1 piece of cinnamon stick or star anise

3 cloves

balsamic vinegar, to taste (optional)

**SERVES 6**

Peel, halve and core the pears (but leave the stalk on for decoration). Put the halves in a saucepan with the sugar, wine and enough water to cover, then add the cinnamon and cloves. Bring slowly to the boil until the sugar dissolves, then reduce the heat and simmer for about 40 minutes or until the pears are tender.

Taste the pear syrup and add a few drops of balsamic vinegar if necessary to correct any excessive sweetness. Leave to cool.

Make up a dessert plate with a few bitter salad leaves, such as radicchio, a generous scoop of soft blue cheese, such as Gorgonzola dolce, a few toasted walnuts and a little of the syrup spooned over the top.

# GRAPE JELLIES

These are an attractive alternative to plain grapes.

2 sheets of leaf gelatine (or 3 – check manufacturer's recommendations for this amount of liquid)
300 ml red grape juice
300 g red or black seedless grapes

*6 small glasses or shot glasses*

**SERVES 6**

Put the gelatine sheets in a shallow dish and sprinkle over 2 tablespoons cold water. Leave to soak for 2–3 minutes. Meanwhile, gently heat the grape juice in a small saucepan until almost boiling. When the gelatine is soft, remove each sheet from the water, add to the grape juice, stir, then leave to cool.

When the jelly is cold, wash the grapes, halving the larger ones. Fill the glasses with the grapes, then top up with the jelly. Cover with clingfilm, put in the fridge and leave to set, pressing the fruit down into the jelly halfway through the setting time.

**See picture on page 142.**

# GEWURZTRAMINER JELLY CUBES

**Gewurztraminer has an exotic flavour that makes a great accompaniment for washed-rinded cheeses like Munster. For a striking effect, make it into a jelly.**

6 small sheets of leaf gelatine
550 ml Gewurztraminer
2–3 tablespoons sugar syrup

**SERVES 6–8**

Put the gelatine sheets in a shallow dish and sprinkle over 3 tablespoons cold water. Leave to soak for 3 minutes. Meanwhile, gently heat the Gewurztraminer in a small saucepan until almost boiling. When the gelatine is soft, remove each sheet from the water and drop them into the saucepan. Remove from the heat and stir until the gelatine has dissolved. Sweeten the liquid jelly to taste with the sugar syrup. Pour the jelly into a shallow rectangular tin, cover and put in the fridge to set for 2 hours.

Cut the jelly into cubes with a sharp knife and serve with cheese.

# SPICED QUINCE COMPOTE WITH RED WINE AND CLOVES

Quinces turn a beautiful jewel-red colour when they are cooked – making this compote a lovely accompaniment for a mellow blue cheese, such as Stilton or Gorgonzola dolce.

2 large or 3 smaller quince
a good squeeze of lemon (about 1 tablespoon)
75 g golden caster sugar
1 cinnamon stick
6 cloves
1 fine strip of orange zest (optional)
250 ml fruity red wine

**SERVES 8–10**

Peel, core and quarter the quince, then cut into even-sized dice. (This is tougher than it sounds – quince are very hard!) As you cut them, put them in a saucepan of acidulated water (i.e. water with a good squeeze of lemon juice) to stop them discolouring.

When you've finished chopping, drain off the water, add the sugar, cinnamon, cloves and orange zest, if using, pour over the red wine and top up with water to cover. Set the pan over low heat and cook, stirring occasionally, until the sugar has dissolved. Bring the syrup up to boiling point, then reduce the heat, half-cover the pan and simmer until the quince is soft (up to 1 hour). You may need to top up the liquid with boiling water so that the quince always remain covered.

Remove the cooked quince pieces from the pan with a slotted spoon and transfer to a bowl. Continue simmering the syrup until it is thick and coats the back of a spoon. Strain it onto the quince, leave to cool and then serve. The compote can be stored in a lidded container in the fridge for up to 1 week.

* You could play around with the spices in this recipe and add 6 lightly crushed cardamom pods or 2 pieces of star anise instead of the cloves.

# LEFTOVER CHEESE

If you have relatively small leftover pieces of cheese, it's better to find some use for them in the kitchen than to store them – see page 151. And there are many tasty options, from cheese on toast (page 69) to pizza toppings (page 111).

You obviously need to check that the cheese is still edible and within its 'use by' date, if it has one. A bit of mould on a hard cheese isn't necessarily a problem (it can be trimmed off) but discard cheeses that have developed brownish patches or that smell in any way unpleasant. And don't take any risks at all if you or the person you're serving it to is pregnant or elderly (see page 4).

My favourite use for leftover bits and pieces is an incredibly easy-to-make cheese spread which the French call 'fromage fort' ('strong cheese'). Simply whizz a couple of cloves of garlic in a food processor, add your sliced-up cheese (having first removed the rinds) and pulse until you have a thick paste. Add just enough white wine to make a spreadable consistency and season with cayenne pepper or chilli powder to taste. For an even stronger version, you could use a splash of eau de vie or brandy. The spread will keep in the fridge for 2–3 days and makes a tasty topping for crackers, crostini or toast. Here are two other simple recipes for leftover cheese.

## WELSH RAREBIT

3 tablespoons full-bodied English ale

75 g strong Cheddar, grated

1½ teaspoons plain flour, sifted

1 egg yolk

¼ teaspoon English mustard

½ teaspoon Worcestershire sauce

1 large or 2 smaller slices of sourdough or country bread

freshly ground black pepper

### SERVES 1

Preheat the grill.

Pour the ale into a saucepan, sprinkle over the Cheddar and flour and stir. Cook over low heat until the cheese has melted and you have a smooth sauce. Remove from the heat and beat in the egg yolk, then add the mustard and Worcestershire sauce. Season with plenty of pepper (you shouldn't need salt).

Grill or toast the bread, then spread with the melted cheese and grill until brown and bubbling.

## STILTON AND PARSLEY BUTTER

100 g unsalted butter, at room temperature

100 g Stilton (weighed with the rind removed)

1 heaped tablespoon finely chopped fresh parsley

sea salt and freshly ground black pepper

### SERVES 8–10

Cut the butter and cheese into small chunks. Place in a bowl and beat together (this is easiest with an electric handheld whisk but you can use a wooden spoon). Season generously with pepper and a pinch of salt and mix in the chopped parsley. Spoon the flavoured butter onto a piece of foil, shaping it into a rectangle. Roll the foil around the cheese to create a cylinder, then twist both ends of the foil like a Christmas cracker and refrigerate until firm.

Remove from the fridge about 20 minutes before serving. It's particularly good with hamburgers or steak.

RIGHT *Welsh Rarebit*

# CHEESE KNOW-HOW

*Finn*

# HOW TO BUY CHEESE

**Although most supermarkets sell an impressive range of cheese these days, and there are some excellent online sites (see page 158), in my view there's nothing to beat buying from a specialist shop or market stall where you can taste the cheese and even talk to the producer.**

In fact with hand-made, artisanal cheese, I would say it's always preferable to buy this way because it changes so much from batch to batch and from season to season. And even a cheese you think you like can be disappointing if it's not been properly looked after – a hazard in some shops that don't rotate their stock sufficiently regularly.

A good shop by contrast may well perform the role of an *affineur* (see page 13), bringing their own cheeses to peak condition. If you shop there regularly, they get to know your tastes and introduce you to new cheeses you might enjoy. The assistants will be able to explain where the cheeses come from, what milk they're made from and what style of cheese they are. They will always cut off a sliver for you to try. They can suggest other cheeses and accompaniments that will complement it or, if you're cooking with it, advise which will work best in the recipe you're planning. The whole experience is a delight, the only downside being the temptation to buy more than you really need or can use before they deteriorate. ('Little and often' or 'buy as you need it' is by far the best counsel when you're buying artisanal cheese.)

The advantage of buying in supermarkets is that quality control is paramount. They're very good at sourcing the most popular cheeses like Cheddar, Camembert and Stilton, where their huge buying power secures them some of the best of what's available.

And they can afford – or twist the producer's arm – to offer them at keener prices than independent shops.

Buying direct from the producer is fun too. I regularly buy from a Somerset cheese maker (White Lake) who takes a stall at my local farmers' market. He specializes in goats' cheese and has some I often buy but I am always amazed at how they vary from batch to batch and season to season. He also experiments with new cheeses, which are always worth trying.

Finally, there's the internet – again tempting – with the online suppliers' wide selection of cheeses and detailed, knowledgeable descriptions. Many of the top cheese shops now have an on-line presence, a boon if you live far from a specialist store. But packaging and transport costs can make them an expensive option.

## ORDERING CHEESE IN A RESTAURANT

Ordering cheese in a restaurant can be intimidating, especially if they trundle around a huge cheese trolley for your inspection, often with cheeses you've never heard of before. Usually a 'cheese sommelier' will run through the options but sometimes there are so many that you forget what they all are. The best way to handle the situation, I find, is to make clear the type of cheeses you prefer and ask which of their cheeses are new, seasonal or locally produced. That way, you taste varieties of cheese you might not have tried before.

# SERVING TEMPERATURES

**Possibly the most important piece of advice in this book is to bring your cheese to cool room temperature before serving it.**

Eating cheese straight from the fridge dumbs down its taste and means that you lose around 50 percent of its flavour. Small cheeses will take a shorter time than whole ones or large pieces of cut cheese. Allow at least 45 minutes and up to 2 hours.

Don't on the other hand let cheese get too warm otherwise it will accentuate its fat content and develop an unpleasantly 'sweaty' consistency – a potential problem during unseasonally hot weather or when you're eating alfresco (see page 71).

**CHEESE TIP**

Don't rule out a style of cheese on the basis of one example you've tried and disliked. Cheeses vary hugely in strength. Even the most pungent washed-rind cheeses and blues have milder versions you might enjoy and there are many goats' cheeses that are not remotely 'goaty'. Do keep tasting and trying!

# CHEESE KNIVES AND BOARDS

A lot of specialist knives are sold for cutting cheese these days. You could theoretically have a different cutter for every type of cheese and indeed some purists do recommend this so that you keep the flavour of each cheese apart. Most of us, however, would settle for two or three knives at most, one round-bladed one for softer cheeses, a sharper one for harder ones and possibly an extra knife for any particularly pungent cheese. I also find a cheese slicer useful for sandwiches.

If you're serving or plating up cheese from the kitchen, you can use ordinary kitchen cutlery. I actually like the effect of using a less than perfectly sharp knife. I don't want my cheese in immaculately straight lines. A couple of dessertspoons are useful for scooping an oval lozenge of soft cheese onto a plate, while a fork will break up a hard cheese into attractively irregular pieces to scatter over a salad. An ordinary vegetable peeler is also useful for getting finer shavings than you can achieve with a purpose-designed cheese slicer.

Other than small round cheeses, which it makes sense to cut into wedges, I don't buy into the idea that cheese should be cut in certain specified ways. People get quite upset if you cut straight across the end of a slice of **Brie**, for example. If that matters to you, I suggest slicing the cheese just before you bring it to the table. That can actually make your cheese board look quite striking, although there is the disadvantage that any unused cheese will dry out more quickly.

The one type of presentation I don't think looks particularly attractive is cutting cheese into cubes or batons. It's hard to do anything else with a block cheese but it rather underlines the fact that your cheese is factory-made rather than artisanal. Maybe that smacks of cheese snobbery but I like cheese to look as natural as possible. Hard cheeses also taste better when they're finely sliced or shaved, rather than chopped, so that they can almost dissolve on the tongue.

## SHOULD YOU REMOVE THE RIND?

I wouldn't remove the rind before serving the cheese course. If the rind is a feature of the cheese, as it is in a washed-rind cheese or a crusted blue like **Stilton**, for example, I would always present it like that at the table, even though my guests might then want to remove it. Indeed I recommend that you do remove the rind once the cheese is on your plate if you think it will interfere with the accompanying wine you're drinking – see page 30.

## CHEESE BOARDS

I like to vary the way I serve cheese depending on the selection. A rustic board can look great with traditional cheeses, such as **Camembert**, **Cheddar** and **Stilton**, but sometimes you can create a more striking effect with a slate (especially with white and white-rinded cheeses), marble or other surfaces (see page 52). A shallow basket lined with vine leaves can also be attractive.

# STORING CHEESE

Cheese is an expensive product so if you're to get the best out of your investment, you need to take care of it once you get it home and plan how you're going to use it. It's too easy to consign it to the fridge and then forget about it.

Store cheese in the warmer part of the fridge (at the top if there isn't a freezer compartment or in an empty salad drawer) as soon as you buy it.

Once cheese is unwrapped it will deteriorate more quickly. At the end of a meal, wrap any remaining cheese and put it away as soon as possible, as it dries out quite easily. Ideally, use waxed paper but if you don't have that, use baking parchment for soft cheese, foil for blues and clingfilm for harder cheese. Each cheese can then be popped into a sealable bag to stop them transmitting and picking up flavours from other ingredients. Very strong-smelling cheeses may need to be wrapped in a damp tea towel and enclosed in a plastic box to prevent their smell pervading the fridge! If you do keep cut cheeses any length of time, you should rewrap them every couple of days.

As a general guide, hard cheeses, whole cheeses and larger pieces of cheese stay fresher longer than soft ones, cut ones and small pieces. And commercial and pasteurized ones keep better than unpasteurized, artisanal ones.

## CAN YOU FREEZE CHEESE?

Purists would say no – the flavour will be affected – but they will be fine for cooking. Mature cheeses tend to freeze better than young cheeses with a high water content, such as **goats' cheese**.

# CHEESE AND HEALTH

**Cheese is a healthy food which contains elements that are an essential part of a balanced diet. You might think that that goes without saying but the idea has got about that cheese is somehow unhealthy either because of the amount of fat it contains, because some people have difficulty tolerating certain cheeses or because of the pasteurization issue.**

I'll touch on these issues below and opposite but let's concentrate on the positives first of all. Cheese is a source of protein, which, as you probably don't need me to tell you, is vital for cell renewal and repair and to keep our bodies functioning healthily; calcium, which is essential for bone and dental health; and essential vitamins, such as A, B12 and D, which assist with good vision, a stable mood and the absorption of calcium respectively.

It's the quantity of cheese you eat that can have deleterious effects. If you're a compulsive snacker, you will certainly put on weight, as you can see opposite, but modest portions (and just 30 g **Cheddar** provides 216 mg calcium) can do nothing but good.

### IS UNPASTEURIZED CHEESE SAFE?

Many of the world's most coveted cheeses are unpasteurized, i.e. made with raw, untreated milk (see page 13). Most of us have no problem with that but if you're pregnant or elderly, the advice is that you should avoid unpasteurized cheeses.

### WHAT IF I'M PREGNANT?

In addition to unpasteurized cheeses, the current view is that uncooked, mould-ripened cheeses, such as **Brie**, **Camembert** and some **goats' cheeses** and **blue cheeses**, should be avoided, as they carry a higher risk of listeria, a bacteria that can be harmful both to the unborn child and anyone with a compromised immune system.

### WHAT IF I'M VEGETARIAN?

Many cheeses are made by adding rennet, an animal-derived substance that comes from the stomachs of calves, which curdles the milk and separates it into curds and whey (see page 11). However, producers often use a similar enzyme from non-animal sources. Cheeses are usually clearly labelled as suitable for vegetarians but if you're unsure, always check with the retailer or cheese producer. Vegans do not eat any animal-derived products so don't offer cheese to a vegan guest.

### WHAT IF I CAN'T TOLERATE COWS' MILK?

People who have a lactose intolerance find that they suffer from bloating, cramps and other symptoms after eating cheese, particularly cows' milk cheese. They lack enough of the enzyme lactase, which breaks down lactose and makes it digestible.

They may find they can eat cheese from other animals, such as sheep, goats and buffalo but these contain lactose too so consult your guests first.

# CUTTING YOUR CHEESE CALORIES

However delicious, cheese is a calorific food. There's no getting away from it, but it's more often the other foods you eat with it that add up to the calorie overload. Bread, biscuits, butter, potatoes, pasta and cream – all the yummy things in life, unfortunately – pile on the pounds if you don't exercise some portion control!

The good news is that there are less indulgent ways to enjoy cheese and that some cheeses are less calorific than others, most notably younger, fresher cheeses that have a higher water content. The list below shows the number of calories per 100 g but bear in mind that a recommended portion size is generally less than a third of that (see below) and that individual cheese recipes vary (artisanal cheeses, for example, tend to be higher in calories than commercial versions).

There are also low-calorie versions of higher-calorie cheeses but I'm never particularly impressed with them. I would always rather enjoy the full-strength versions and eat slightly less of them.

## LOW-FAT CHEESES (PER 100 G)

Young, soft cheeses
**Cottage cheese**: 114 calories
**Low-fat fromage frais**: 50 calories
**Fresh goats' cheese**: 160 calories (but goats' cheese logs are higher in calories)
**Quark**: 66 calories
**Ricotta**: 134 calories

## MEDIUM-FAT CHEESES (PER 100 G)

White-rinded and Greek cheeses
**Brie**: 296 calories
**Camembert**: 283 calories
**Feta**: 262 calories
**Halloumi**: 315 calories
**Mozzarella**: 274 calories

## HIGHER-FAT CHEESES (PER 100 G)

Hard cheeses and those with added cream
**Mature Cheddar**: 416 calories
**Gruyère**: 409 calories
**Pecorino**: 397 calories
**Stilton**: 412 calories
**Mascarpone**: 435 calories
**Parmesan**: 401 calories

## A LOW-FAT CHEESE AND ONION DIP

To make a low-fat cheese dip, use **quark**, one of the lowest-calorie cheeses on the market with about 66 calories per 100 g. Mix a 250-g tub with about 125 ml semi-skimmed or skimmed milk to create a smooth, dipping consistency. Add ½ small onion, very finely chopped, a crushed garlic clove, ½ teaspoon sea salt and a dash of Tabasco green pepper sauce.

## WATCH YOUR PORTION SIZE!

As you can see, it's not so much that all cheese is highly calorific, rather it's the amount of it we eat. It's also worth keeping consumption in check because cheese is high in saturated fats.

On most weight-control programmes, a recommended portion for a hard cheese is 30 g and slightly more (40 g) for a soft, lower-fat cheese. That might not sound a lot but it will seem more generous if you cut or shave it finely, grate it or crumble it, rather than serving it as a single piece.

## CUTTING YOUR CARBS

Another strategy is to cut out (or reduce) any accompanying carbohydrates in the form of bread or crackers. The French typically eat their cheese on its own when they're having it during a meal (a picnic is another matter when the customary baguette is a must!)
If you can't do without, there are now many elegant alternatives to the rather spartan crispbreads that used to be the rule: low-fat, seed-topped flatbreads and crisp Sardinian carta da musica being two of my favourites. And think in terms of open Scandinavian-style sandwiches rather than the normal double-sided ones (see page 75). Even for a party you can hand round canapés based on fruits and vegetables rather than bread, biscuit or pastry bases or serve them on cocktail sticks. Here are some ideas using low-fat cheeses.
◆ Sticks of celery filled with tarragon-flavoured **quark**
◆ Thick slices of cucumber topped with **quark** or **fromage frais** and smoked salmon (you can adapt the ideas for the verrines on page 88)
◆ Cherry tomatoes, split and filled with **low-fat soft cheese**, flavoured with a dash of Tabasco
◆ Watermelon and **Feta** kebabs
◆ Greek salad on a stick: a cube of **Feta**, a cherry tomato, a square of cucumber and a black olive
◆ Halved fresh figs topped with creamy **blue cheese**

# QUICK CHEESE AND WINE MATCHER

As you will have already seen, there are many alternative suggestions for drink pairings in the section on What to Drink with Cheese (see pages 28–47) but if you're looking for a match for a specific cheese, here's a brief summary to make your task quicker. Do remember though that the age and condition of the cheese and the accompaniments you pair with it will make a difference.

**Appenzeller**: Swiss white wines, schnapps

**Beaufort**: Wines from the Savoie region of France, dry amontillado sherry, aged tawny port, bière ambrée

**Brie**: Soft fruity reds, such as cru Beaujolais and Pinot Noir, fruity rosés, raspberry- and cherry-flavoured beers, Guignolet, Japanese plum wine

**Brillat-Savarin**: Champagne and other sparkling wine, apricot brandy

**Cabrales**: sweet oloroso sherry, Bual and Malmsey Madeira, Malaga

**Caerphilly**: Cava or still Xarel-lo, Gavi di Gavi, English Bacchus, Côtes du Rhone

**Camembert**: Cider, Pommeau, Calvados, Oregon or New Zealand Pinot Noir

**Cantal**: Port, Rhone reds such as Gigondas and Chateauneuf du Pape, Biere de garde

**Cashel Blue**: *See* Stilton. You could also try an Irish Malt whisky.

**Chaource**: Chablis and Champagne

**Cheddar**: Vintage port, medium-dry cider, English ales, oak-aged beers, barrel-aged Chardonnay, sherry cask-aged whisky

**Cheshire**: red Bordeaux, Bergerac, cider, apple juice

**Comté**: Vin jaune, dry amontillado sherry, white Bordeaux

**Epoisses**: Sauternes, strong Belgian beers, Marc de Bourgogne or Marc de Champagne, Genever

**Feta**: Greek white wines, such as Assyrtiko, ouzo

**Fourme d'Ambert**: 'Porty' reds, such as Zinfandel, Negroamaro, Bandol, port

**Gaperon**: Crisp dry whites, and simple rustic French reds, such as Marcillac

**Goats' cheese**: Sauvignon Blanc is the outstanding match. English whites, German Kabinett or dry Alsace Riesling, witbier, apple schnapps and elderflower cordial are all good.

**Gorgonzola**: Passito di Pantelleria, Vin Santo, Amarone

**Gouda**: Tempranillo-based reds, Argentine Malbec, dry amontillado sherry, tawny port

**Gruyère**: Amontillado and dry oloroso sherry, 20-year-old tawny port, smoked beer, sake

**Lancashire**: Traditional English ales. Mature Spanish, Southern French or South Italian reds.

LEFT *(From top) Gorgonzola, Perroche, Manchego (from left to right: 6, 7–9, 9–12 and 14 months old)*

**Lincolnshire Poacher**: Full-bodied English ales and barley wines

**Manchego and other hard sheep's cheeses**: Rioja and other Tempranillo-based reds, Roussanne and Marsanne-based whites, fino sherry, dry madeira, quince-flavoured liqueurs, sake

**Maroilles**: Trappist beers, such as Chimay Bleue, eaux de vie

**Mimolette**: Red Bordeaux and other Cabernet-Merlot blends

**Morbier**: Spanish reds, such as Rioja

**Mozzarella**: Rarely eaten without accompanying ingredients, usually tomato. Best served with dry Italian whites or, as a pizza topping, with fruity Italian reds.

**Munster**: Gewurztraminer, sweet Alsace or German Riesling, plum-flavoured eaux de vie, Belgian and Northern French beers

**Ossau-Iraty**: South-western French and Languedoc reds, such as Madiran and Corbières. Dry southern French or Spanish rosé. Sweet Jurançon and Pacherenc du Vic-Bilh from the same region, bières ambrées and dry cider.

**Parmesan (Parmigiano-Reggiano)**: Classic, medium-bodied reds, such as Bordeaux and Chianti, Champagne and similar sparkling wines, Maury and Banyuls

**Pecorino**: Italian reds, Poire William

**Pont-l'Evêque**: Sparkling cider, Pommeau, Calvados or other apple brandies, aromatic whites, such as Alsace Pinot Gris

**Reblochon**: Pinot Gris from Alsace, Trappist beers, marc

**Roquefort**: Sauternes and similar sweet Bordeaux, peaty Islay whiskies, such as Lagavulin

**Stilton/Stichelton**: Sweet red wines, such as port, elderberry wine, sloe gin, tawny port, sweet sherry, Tokaji, barley wines, peaty whiskies, mead

**Stinking Bishop**: Somerset Cider Brandy, strong apple or pear aperitifs and digestifs, scrumpy (West Country cider), barley wine

**Taleggio**: Franciacorta sparkling wine, Arneis, Grüner Veltliner, Barbera

**Tête de Moine**: Rich, oak-aged Chardonnay, Côtes de Rhône Villages, amber ales, dry, nutty sherries

**Tomme de Savoie**: Crisp, dry whites from the Savoie region, dry Riesling

**Torta del Casar**: Aged Rioja, Cava Reserva

**Vacherin Mont d'Or**: Champagne (especially vintage Champagne), crisp dry whites from Switzerland and the Savoie region of France

**Valençay**: Loire whites, such as Quincy, Menetou-Salon and Sancerre (or other mineral, cool-climate Sauvignon Blancs), mature Alsace Riesling

**Wensleydale**: English whites, wheat beer, Côtes du Rhone

# CHEESE GLOSSARY

**Cheese aficionados tend to use a special vocabulary which can sometimes be confusing to ordinary mortals. Here's what they're talking about:**

**Affineur**: Literally a 'cheese maturer' – a craftsman who takes cheeses from a producer and brings them to perfect maturity (see page 13). They usually have their own shops.

**Aged cheese**: Cheeses that are deliberately matured to develop their flavour. Parmesan and Gruyère are common examples. Sometimes referred to as 'cave-aged', simply meaning this process has been carried out in a cellar.

**Alpine cheese**: Synonym for the semi-hard cheeses that are made in the Alpine regions of France Switzerland and Italy, such as Gruyère, Emmental and the various tommes and tomas. A broader description than 'Swiss cheese', which refers more specifically to Emmental-style cheeses.

**Artisanal cheese**: A hand-made cheese made on a farm or by a small producer from locally sourced milk.

**Block cheese**: Industrially produced hard cheeses produced in large amounts. Usually used of Cheddar. The shape may be uninspiring but the flavour can be perfectly good.

**Bloomy-rinded**: The sort of white, velvety rind you find on cheeses, such as Brie and Camembert and some goats' cheeses. Also known as white-rinded.

**Curds**: The solid portion of the milk that remains when it is separated from the liquid whey following the addition of rennet or other coagulant (see page 11).

**Dutch cheese**: Gouda or Gouda-style cheeses (see page 21)

**Farmhouse cheese**: Rather loosely used as a marketing term but should strictly refer to cheeses that have been produced on a farm by the owner of the animals in question.

**Fresh**: Fresh as in young, rather than fresh as opposed to stale. Commonly used of soft, unrinded, spreadable cheeses, especially young goats' and sheep's cheeses.

**Mould**: Sounds unappetizing but does not necessarily mean mouldy. The mould may have been deliberately introduced to develop the flavour of the cheese as in a blue cheese (see page 22).

**Mould-ripened**: Another description for bloomy-rinded cheeses. such as Brie and Camembert.

**Natural-rinded**: Natural-rinded cheeses are those which develop a rind simply by being exposed to the air. (Unlike washed-rind cheeses, the rind is not washed or treated.) In practice, this term is mainly used of goats' cheeses that have been allowed to mature and develop a greyish, wrinkled rind. As the cheese becomes dryer, the flavour becomes more intense. The French cheese Crottin de Chavignol is a good example.

**Paste**: The centre of the cheese, inside the rind casing.

**Pasteurized**: Cheese that has been heat-treated to prevent bacterial growth.

**Raw-milk cheese**: Unpasteurized cheese made from untreated milk.

**Rind**: The surface that develops over a matured cheese which may be hard, 'bloomy' (see above) or slightly sticky, as in a washed-rind cheese.

**Semi-hard cheese**: Confusingly used in different ways by different experts. Some consider any cheese which is not well aged and crumbly like a Parmesan to be 'semi-hard' and would categorize Cheddar this way. Others – including me – use the term to refer to cheeses, such as Gruyère and Gouda that are firm but still have some pliability.

**Semi-soft cheese**: Cheeses that are sliceable but which have a flexible, bendable consistency. Most washed-rind cheeses, such as Munster and Reblochon, are semi-soft, as are Camembert and Brie, although they are seldom described this way.

**Swiss cheese**: General description for Emmental-style cheeses that have holes in the paste.

**Washed-rind cheese**: Cheeses whose surface is washed or rubbed with a salt water solution or with wine, beer, cider or marc to develop their flavour, e.g. Epoisses, and Stinking Bishop.

## TASTING TERMS

**Barnyardy/Farmyardy**: Terms often used of a well matured washed-rind cheese, for obvious reasons.

**Buttery**: Often used of creamy cows' milk cheeses, such as Brillat-Savarin or Explorateur.

**Citrussy**: The fresh, light notes you tend to find in young goats' cheeses and delicately flavoured cheeses, such as Chaource.

**Fruity**: The complex flavours you tend to find in Alpine cheese, such as Comté and Beaufort, which reflect the flavours of the floral- and herb-rich pastures on which the animals graze.

**Mushroomy**: A term often used of Brie and similar cheeses which can often taste of raw mushrooms.

**Nutty**: Used of aged cheeses, such as Cheddar, Gouda and Gruyère.

**Piquant**: Used of cheeses that have a pronounced savoury sharpness or 'bite', such as aged Parmesan.

**Pungent**: An alternative word for strong (and occasionally stinky).

**Ripe**: A cheese that has reached its peak of flavour (usually after careful maturation).

**Sharp**: A positive attribute in a cheese, indicating well-defined flavours. Often used of Cheddar and blues, such as Roquefort.

**Stinky**: *See* Barnyardy.

**Strong**: A cheese with a more pronounced flavour than is typical of its type, as in a 'strong' Cheddar.

*ABOVE (From left) Double Gloucester, buffalo Mozzarella, Parmesan, aged Pecorino, Colston Bassett Stilton, cheese grater, Strachitunt, button of goats' cheese (top) and Charolais goats' cheese (below)*

# CHEESE SUPPLIERS AND WEBSITES

### UK

**The Fine Cheese Co.**
29 & 31 Walcot Street
Bath
BA1 5BN
Telephone: 01225 483407
www.finecheese.co.uk
*Chic cheese shop with clever
selections and accompaniments.*

**La Fromagerie**
2–6 Moxon Street
London
W1U 4EW
Telephone: 020 7935 0341
www.lafromagerie.co.uk
*Fabulous boutique cheese shop,
cheese room and café with branches
in Marylebone and Highbury.*

**La Cave à Fromage**
24–25 Cromwell Place
London
SW7 2LD
Telephone: 020 7581 1804

www.la-cave.co.uk
*French-style cheese shop with branches
in South Kensington and Brighton.*

**Neal's Yard Dairy**
17 Shorts Gardens
London
WC2H 9UP
Telephone: 020 7240 5700
www.nealsyarddairyshop.co.uk
*Mouth-watering selection of British
and Irish cheeses. Branches in
Borough Market and Covent Garden.*

**Paxton & Whitfield**
93 Jermyn Street
London
SW1Y 6JE
Telephone: 020 7930 0259
www.paxtonandwhitfield.co.uk

*Ultra-traditional Dickensian Piccadilly
shop with a very up-to-date,
accessible website. Other branches in
Bath and Stratford-upon-Avon.*

### IRELAND

**Sheridans**
11 South Anne Street
Dublin 2
Telephone: 01 679 3143
www.sheridanscheesemongers.com
*Tiny jewel of a Dublin cheese shop
with branches in Galway and
Waterford.*

### FRANCE

**Bernard Antony**
*Superb Alsace-based cheese affineur,
supplier to many of France's 3-star
Michelin restaurants.*
http://pagesperso-orange.fr/
fromagerieantony/Fromager.htm

**Fromages.com**
*French-based, English language*

*website with a large selection of
French cheeses.*
www.fromages.com

**Marie-Anne Cantin**
*Top Parisian* affineur *and cheese shop.*
www.cantin.fr

**Rodolphe Le Menier (Tours)**
*Innovative* affineur *and cheese shop.*
www.fromages-en-jazz.com

### FOR MORE INFORMATION

**The Cheeselover**
*My regular cheese blog!*
http://thecheeselover.blogspot.com

**American Cheese Society**
*Main organization representing
American cheese makers and retailers.*
www.cheesesociety.org

**British Cheese Board**
*Promotional body for British cheese.*
www.britishcheese.com

**French Cheese**
*An A–Z of French cheeses.*
www.frenchcheese.co.uk

**Specialist Cheesemakers Association**
*Comprehensive listing of British-based
cheese makers and shops.*
www.specialistcheesemakers.co.uk

**Australian Specialist Cheesemakers'
Association**
*A similar site for Australian cheeses.*
www.australiancheese.org

The publisher would like to thank
**Summerill & Bishop** for the kind loan
of the glass domes on pages 2–3.
Visit their shop at:
100 Portland Road
London W11 4LN
Telephone: 020 7221 4566
www.summerillandbishop.com

# INDEX